D0007945

9000948967

4/6

WHAT GOD
CAN DO

ALSO BY DEBORAH MATHIS

Yet a Stranger:
Why Black Americans Still Don't Feel at Home

What God Can Do

How Faith Changes Lives
for the Better

Deborah Mathis

ATRIA BOOKS

NEW YORK   LONDON   TORONTO   SYDNEY

ATRIA BOOKS
1230 Avenue of the Americas
New York, NY 10020

ISBN: 0-7434-7640-9

First Atria Books hardcover edition June 2005

10   9   8   7   6   5   4   3   2   1

ATRIA BOOKS is a trademark of Simon & Schuster, Inc.

Manufactured in the United States of America

For information regarding special discounts for bulk purchases,
please contact Simon & Schuster Special Sales at 1-800-456-6798
or business@simonandschuster.com

For struggling and striving believers everywhere.

Acknowledgments

As I embarked upon the research and planning for this book, my mind crawled with memories of people I had come across in my fifty years and the stories they told that involved some special favor from God. Putting names and faces to all of the stories was the first challenge. Honing down this library of remembrances to manageable size was the next. Tracking down the principals was one of the toughest jobs. But getting them to talk was a piece of cake.

I am grateful to the many men and women who gave their time—hours and hours in some cases—to this project and who entrusted me with their very personal testimonies. In interview after interview, they poured their hearts and souls out: Marsha Allen, Matthew Bishop, Wilbert Burgess, Millie Carter, Carla Hardeman, Jason Mathis, Dee McClendon, Mabel Mitchell, Steve Nawojczyk. I wish to thank them for their candor and cooperation. I am honored by their faith in my attempt to do justice to their stories and the spiritual faith those stories exemplify.

I am also indebted to the good friends who helped dig out names, numbers, and dates for me, particularly my soul mate and friend Karyne Jones and the fabulous Shirley Davis, a woman with a heart of gold and a singing voice that uplifts, inspires, and sometimes blows a few minds.

I must certainly bow to Atria Books for giving me an opportunity to talk about what God can do. I'm especially grateful to my editor, Malaika Adero, for her patience and generosity from start to finish. As always, I have to give it up to Caroline Carney, my former literary agent and great friend who kept me encouraged no matter what.

I thank, too, my family—Rachel Myers and C. J. Jones, my mother and stepfather, who gave me peace, comfort, and the run of their Florida home while writing this book; my sister and brother-in-law, Sandra and Anderson Hill, who ran interference for me when finances and logistics threatened to distract me; my brothers, John and Lloyd Myers, who infected me with their contagious confidence in this project; and my three best friends—Meredith, Allison, and Joseph: my children don't seem to know when to stop with the hugs, the smiles, the assistance, and the compliments.

Surely some of these good people must have wondered, at times, how I got to be so audacious as to attempt a book on God and faithfulness, given the aggravation, self-pity, frustration, and self-centeredness I frequently exhibited while writing the book. But if they doubted, they never said it and they never showed it. They are all my angels.

And what can I say about God? Suffice it to say that nothing can adequately express how grateful I am for this opportunity, how I hope I have pleased Him and how thankful I am that He keeps giving me "second" chances. God is great and God is good.

Contents

CONTENTS

Introduction

Having grown up as a "P.K."—a preacher's kid—many of my memories and much of my perspective stand against the backdrop of religion, spirituality, and church. God was always a part of our family life and His presence was continually beseeched and praised. Even as we were enveloped in segregation and massive, chancy social change, the six of us—mother, father, two daughters followed by two sons—enjoyed a very good life. My parents were conspicuously in love with each other; modeled respect and admiration for each other; had good-paying, respectable careers; and treated us kids as treasures. Through their due diligence, we had most of what we wanted and everything we needed, including a rich reserve of values, standards, and wisdom to shepherd us through times good and bad.

Still, I am a product of, more than anything else, grace. Were it not for that, my story might have a decidedly different bent—a tale of dark shadows, tragedy, and deprivation. For despite the many advantages I had, I still managed to find and nurture a rather devilish part of my nature, and that indulgence took me to the edge many times. I have never been shot or stabbed, never been in a serious car accident, never been seriously ill, never been incarcerated, never been homeless, never been truly down and out. However, I frequently traveled down an ominous old road that ended in trouble and danger—a popular, wanton path from which countless sojourners have not safely traveled or returned. For some reason, I was spared their woeful fate and, as they say, have lived to tell about it. That reason, I now know, is the forgiveness, patience, and love—the consummate mercy—of God.

For whatever it's worth, I never engaged in risky behavior as conscious rebellion or in reckless or purposeful disregard for anything or anyone. I hadn't tried to hurt and frighten my parents, but now I know I did. I hadn't intended to put my own survival, health, and future in jeopardy, but now I know I did. I hadn't wanted to flout God and righteousness, but now I know I did. Looking back, I realize my life, like all others, has been a series of near misses, and that many of those hazards were of my own making. So I am living proof of the old adage that God takes care of fools.

More than that, I am living proof that God can make use of even us prodigals. I have understood that for a long time, yet I was still surprised when, one night, I was tapped for duty. There I was, minding my own business, when something inside me announced that it was time to write a book that would attempt some modicum of homage and witness to God's goodness. The "assignment," if you will, came replete with a title for the book: *What God Can Do.*

Of course, I recognized the title immediately from an old song

I had learned as a kid. I was a little girl attending Vacation Bible School at Mount Zion Baptist Church in Little Rock, Arkansas, when I first heard the now-familiar refrain, "It is no secret what God can do." The song was written by Stuart Hamblin, a radio and movie personality popular in the first decades of the twentieth century. The song was a hit off the bat. "It Is No Secret What God Can Do" was recorded by such legends as Elvis Presley, the Jordanaires, Kate Smith, and Mahalia Jackson.

I fell in love with that song, partly because it was so different from the hymns and spirituals and old gospel music I was accustomed to. By comparison, it seemed more modern, sweeter, happier than the usual fare. There was something accessible, something uncomplicated, something plain about it. I loved the melody at once. As the years wore on, I also came to appreciate the simple but honest lyrics.

The book, I decided, would be like the song—not a religious rant, and not demagogic. How could it be otherwise, coming from me, struggling Christian that I am? Certainly I respect the plethora of spiritual works from people who have led circumspect lives, and the goodness, hope, and resolve they have inspired in readers is admirable indeed.

But I am not qualified to write that kind of book. I sin too much, doubt too much, wonder too much, slip too often to even feign consecration. I am too vain, too temperamental, too weak to pull off such a pretense with any credibility whatsoever. If it was to be a genuine and honest report, then I knew that *What God Can Do* would have to come from ground level—ordinary people's accounts of the trials and triumphs of their lives, their testimonies about what God can do.

Therefore, *What God Can Do* is comprised of real-life accounts of the little things that happen to save us, cure us, comfort us, encourage and inspire us, and deliver us from evil. Although I had been mesmerized and moved early in life by the ancient miracles—the parting of the Red Sea, the conversion of water into wine, the raising of the dead, making the blind man see—I have since come to recognize God's handiwork in more ordinary ways and to appreciate those as every bit as wondrous as the major miracles of religious lore.

Thus, this book provides a sampling of soft and subtle miracles of deliverance, the stuff that we often chalk up to coincidence or strokes of luck but which, upon closer examination, defy mortal logic and explanation. I wanted to inspire readers to look for, expect, and find God in ordinary circumstances and to take comfort in knowing that even when no vast sea is divided by an unseen wall, even when no momentous cause is being served, even when no masses of chosen people are being liberated, He is working; His eye is on the sparrow.

What God Can Do contains but a few examples from my life and those of people I know and know of. No publisher would take on a book big enough to account for every blessing of which I am aware. It would make *War and Peace* look like a cover page.

The stories that follow are true accounts from people who knew then or at least know now that particular "coincidences" or "lucky breaks" in their lives—or a series of them—were, in fact, divine orchestrations. Some of the stories come from people who have been faithfully striving all of their lives to please God. But others come from those who, like me, have faltered in the faith or, in some cases, had turned their backs on God.

Even before I began my research for the book, I had stored away many of these stories in fond memory, using them as a private source of inspiration and perseverance. And even before I learned the empirical evidence of a surge in spirituality and religious want in America, I sensed what author John Kirvan calls "God hunger." Without any surveys or studies to back them up, my instincts told me that our country and world cannot incuriously and dispassionately abide the cycle of murder, mayhem, greed, avarice, and deceit. I knew we craved relief, rescue, refuge, something to hold on to, a return to what works, a higher power.

At the same time, I appreciate the frailty of faith in divine power. After all, we modern folks are such creatures of reason, logic, and technology that it strains us to put stock in something so vaporous as faith. Some of us are intimidated by the very idea of it.

I believe the stories recalled in this book may allay some of those doubts. I hope readers will find something to identify with, something that strikes a familiar chord so they will see God's wonders at work in lives like theirs. Maybe the stories will prompt someone to reexamine his or her experiences and circumstances, and help them recognize the distinguishing characteristics of God's touch. Maybe they will find relief in knowing what He's done for others and, thereby, what He can do for us, even if we have been lax in our faith. I want to demonstrate the comfort of His presence, the joy of His love, the boundlessness of His amazing grace and mercy. I want to help readers develop an eye for the evidence of God's little finger in the days of our lives.

If it has been a secret what God can do, may these stories help solve the riddle. May they show that miracles do happen. And that, while God can still raise the dead and make the blind to see, He has other ways of blessing us. And that sometimes, those ways do not become apparent until we have gone through trials—into dungeons, through pain and tragedy, at the brink of death itself. And that when the blessing comes into fullness, we can look back and know that "how I got over" was not by "lucking out," but by a feat of grace.

Rest assured that I present these stories without an iota of sanctimony. I am humbled by the assignment I got that night and grateful for the opportunity to publish this book. And if anyone is amazed that I have taken on this project, they cannot be more so than I. This project has been a detour from my usual domain—politics and social policy. As a commentator in those arenas, I have been accused of being a know-it-all. But, rest assured, I suffer no illusions about my spiritual aptitude. From the beginning, I realized that researching and writing this book, while hard work, would be a learning adventure, a labor of discovery and enlightenment.

In their willing and candid recollections, the men and women who shared their stories with me helped renew and underscore my faith. They helped move me closer to that place I so desperately long to be—in the camp of those who please God. Still, as the poet said, "there are miles to go . . ."

I can say this much, however: Because of this work, I no longer think in terms of happenstance and fortuity. Thanks to this assignment, I no longer say "by coincidence." Now I know, it's "by God." Now I know that "what God can do" is not merely a lovely lyric. It is a delicious wonder.

PART ONE

❦

Heal, Shield,

and Fortify

1

Standing on the Promises

Normally, in the middle of a summer day, all the action would be on the sidewalk, where the neighborhood children gathered for hopscotch or jump rope or hanging around swapping bits of gossip about childhood crushes or feuds or So-and-so's run-in with his grandmother's switch right there in the middle of the grocery store for all the world to see. The street per se was usually quiet and empty; most of the traffic flow was confined to residents' comings and goings in the long or chunky sedans they kept in driveways, carports, and garages that hugged their houses. So, of course we noticed the row of cars parked along the curb in front of our house. Only visitors parked on the street.

"Looks like ya'll have company," the lady said as she slowed the heavy, rumbling sedan to a stop.

"Yes ma'am," I answered, nudging my little sister who was beginning to doze off under the summer heat. We grabbed our little Vacation Bible School workbooks and bid our carpool driver adieu.

Curious looks passed between Sandra and me as we scanned the strange line of cars. Only one was familiar: the shiny brown Lincoln that belonged to our favorite grown-up in the whole wide world—our mother's first cousin, our lively, beloved Janet. We could never get enough of Janet, a first-grade teacher with a transparent love and an honest-to-goodness respect for children. Although we lived in the same city, we didn't see her as often as we should have or wanted to, but when we did, she always left the impression that she could never tire of us, not even if our frisky little selves showed up on her doorstep every day.

The truth was, however, that Janet usually only came to our house on special occasions, like when some out-of-town guests were staying with us. About the only other time she came was when something was wrong.

My sister and I flew up the twenty-one steps that scaled the long, green terrace leading to our front lawn. Rounding the house, we raced through the back door, past the den and the kitchen, slowing only as we approached the living room with its muffled, grown-up voices emanating from behind closed doors.

Easing into the room, I found my mother seated on the sofa, a handkerchief pressed to her cheek. The loving and lovable Janet sat next to her with one arm draped around her shoulders.

Mr. Fowler, the principal at Rightsell Elementary School where Mama taught first grade, was sitting in the stuffed swivel chair nearby, pipe clenched in his teeth, elbows resting on his knees, head bowed.

Two strangers stood near the piano—very strange strangers, I thought. One was a woman in a nun's habit, the other, a man in a long white doctor's coat. The nun looked sweetly sorrowful with her hands clasped below her waist. The man in the doctor's coat looked perturbed. He rubbed his brow so hard I thought he was going to pull the skin off.

My nine-year-old brain burned with worry and confusion. Then dread. Somehow I knew the scene had something to do with my father, who had been in the hospital for three days for something called "elective surgery"—an operation he chose to have, not one he needed. At least that's what we had been told.

A doctor? A nun? Mama crying? Janet consoling? Mr. Fowler not his usual outgoing, smiling self? We had been assured that Daddy's operation was no big deal, that he would be fine and home soon. But what I saw that day said otherwise.

I tiptoed into the room and gingerly took a seat next to my mother. My eyes drifted from her to Janet to Mr. Fowler. Nothing.

"M-m-mama?" I stammered, my heart racing. "What's wrong?"

Mama lifted her sweet face, dabbing at the tears.

"Hi, baby," she said tenderly. "You doing okay?" Her pretty brown eyes swam in tears and her voice was weak.

"Mama, what's wrong?" I repeated, almost breathlessly. Beyond the door, I heard Sandra begin to cry.

"San, you can come in, sweetheart," Mama called out. "Everything's all right. Daddy's just got to be in the hospital a little longer than we thought. It's going to be all right, okay? Do you believe me?"

We nodded out of respect for our mother and to encourage her . . . and ourselves.

"The doctor is just explaining what's going on, but your daddy is going to be fine," Mama explained, brushing my brow and hair, then Sandra's. "Let us finish talking and I'll be in there in a minute." She smiled and hugged us both.

Sweet, sweet woman. Mama was so gentle and good, good to the bone. She practically never lost her temper or her calm. She never cussed and almost never cried. But she had a tough core. As a black woman born into the Depression-era Jim Crow South, she needed one. If ever there was a "steel magnolia," it was she.

Sandra and I retired to the den and its console TV. I turned the knob and located one of our favorite shows. Sandra dutifully plopped down and stared at the screen. Yet I knew that, like mine, Sandra's mind was on the living room and on Daddy.

After a few minutes, I slipped from my sister's side and took refuge in the bathroom, locking the door and turning on the faucet. Holding on to the basin, I lowered myself to my knees and clasped my free hand over my mouth to stifle the full-throated sobs I could no longer suppress.

God, I don't know what's wrong, but I know something is wrong with Daddy. Please, God. Please don't let him be too sick. Please don't let him die. If you have never heard me before, please hear me this time. We need Daddy. He is such a good man. Please, God. Please make everything all right.

To this day, I can recall the utter helplessness I felt in those moments in the bathroom with the water running. I was a young Christian, having been baptized only the year before, and I had only a fledgling knowledge of and faith in God. Would He really listen to a nine-year-old on her knees in the bathroom of a rambler on Twenty-first Street in Little Rock, Arkansas? Could my urgent and simple plea get through all the wails of starving children, of war-torn lands, of poor people, of presidents and prime ministers with a world to run? Was there something more profound to say? Should I have quoted Scripture in the prayer? Should I have promised something in exchange for the grace I sought?

And would God hold it against me that, at the same time I cried out to Him, a part of me was wondering if He really existed at all? Lord knows, I wanted to believe it, especially then. My mind was a scramble of thoughts. The man in the long white coat was obviously the doctor Mama talked about. Yet judging from the look on his face, the solemnity of his voice, he was at a loss of what to do. Janet was a comforter, but she couldn't heal. Mr. Fowler was a good friend to the family, but his bowed head had been a discouraging sign. And Mama, a woman of great faith and resolve, was clearly in distress. God was all I had left. Please God. Please, be there.

Sandra tapped lightly on the bathroom door. "Deb," she said sniffling. "Are you coming out?"

I don't know how long I had been frozen in those tiny quarters, but it had obviously been long enough to rouse my little sister's suspicions and worry. I shut off the water and swallowed hard to steady my voice. "I'm coming out now," I said, hoping I sounded normal.

Sandra stood at the door with rosy cheeks propping up her wide but fearful eyes. She had news. "I think the man and the Sister are leaving now," she said. She stared at my face as if for answers. "Are you crying?" she asked.

"Naw, girl," I said. "Some of Mr. Fowler's pipe smoke got in my eyes and I had to wash it out. There's nothing to cry about. I asked God to make everything all right and He will."

Just then, Mama and Janet entered the kitchen.

"You all hungry?" Janet asked, already tinkering in the stove.

"Let's get you something to eat," Mama chimed.

Sandra and I strode into the kitchen, relieved by the women's pleasantness and calm. Soon, we were singing and laughing and telling stories about our morning in Vacation Bible School at the beautiful and grand Mount Zion Baptist Church, where I was determined to become one of the big girls in the Intermediate Department. That night, I prayed hard and long again. I asked God to forgive me if I was pestering Him. I still didn't know what the real situation was with my father. But I knew that, whatever it was, we were going to need God's help.

When Daddy came home from the hospital a few days after the living room episode, we were happy to see that he looked perfectly normal. In fact, he looked more rested and robust than before.

Our father was a handsome man to begin with. With dark, wavy hair that dipped into a widow's peak at his forehead and slid into sideburns on either side of his face. With his trim mustache, fair complexion, and a tall, sturdy build, he was a looker. He had, however, a deeper beauty.

Daddy was not only a Baptist minister and Bible scholar, but a student of the classics from Socrates to Shakespeare, and he often entertained congregations with masterful blends of literature and gospel. He was a lover and writer of poetry, a great storyteller, and was known for his intellectual curiosity, genial nature, his wicked butter pound cakes—made from scratch and hand-whipped—and a gift for gardening that, more than once, landed him on a local television evening newscast. He was what I would have called a "Renaissance man" had I known the term at the time.

My father's refinement was unlikely given his upbringing. He was born in 1926 in a country hamlet tucked behind a stretch of state highway in north central Arkansas. We used to joke that Blackwell, Arkansas, was so small, it couldn't even cross the road. The townspeople shared a community well that, as children from homes with running water aplenty, we delighted in as a novelty on our visits "up home."

Daddy's father, Oscar, was a railroad man. In his youth, he hand-laid ties along the Missouri Pacific line as it snaked into the Show Me State. My grandmother, Roxanne, was what would now be called a "housewife" or "homemaker," but the term is far too genteel and nebulous for rural women like her who could hardly have done anything else given that they had no marketable skills and, even if they had, there was no industry around. Just a smattering of corner stores and trading posts, usually staffed by the proprietor's kin. Besides, the work of birthing and rearing babies, stewing laundry, coaxing a struggling garden, and cooking over woodstoves were completely consuming affairs.

Daddy was the sixth of seven surviving children born to Oscar and Roxanne. Two others had died at birth or in infancy. The little house the family shared was crammed with second-hand furniture, and the front room walls were covered in colorful newsprint—the family's rendition of wallpaper.

Life in the tiny, dusty town was a series of small dramas that, at the time, were shrugged off as the cost of living in a time when the nation was between world wars and grappling with momentous change—most notably, mechanization and a nascent civil rights awareness if not yet a movement.

One such drama occurred one day when my father, at age nine, went squirrel hunting for the family's supper. A hunting mate, another young boy, had tripped on a fallen tree branch and his rifle had discharged. The bullet struck my father in his thigh. As my uncle Lacy recalled it, he came home from school that day to find his older brother stretched out on a bed, a bloodied bandage around his leg.

"Your brother got shot today," Grandmother declared, as she slapped biscuit dough in the tiny kitchen. Taking advantage of his little brother's shock and horror, Daddy pretended to be dead. He lay stiff and still as Lacy jostled him and called his name in growing desperation. When the boy grew hysterical, my father jumped up and screamed, terrifying Lacy, who fled in fright.

Daddy never saw a doctor about the wound. There were no hospitals or clinics nearby, not that the family would have had a way to get there or means to pay for medical attention anyway. Grandmother had poured turpentine on the wound and wrapped it tightly in clean cotton to stem the bleeding. That would have to do. And it did. The bullet resided in Daddy's body for the rest of his life.

Not long after the United States entered World War II, Daddy enlisted in the U.S. Marine Corps. He was only sixteen, but he told the recruiters he was older and was signed up on the spot, a ruse that was facilitated by the shoddy, easily altered birth certificate common to poor black southerners of the day, as well as the country's need for servicemen. He served his entire tour at Camp Lejeune, North Carolina, and was honorably discharged at the rank of corporal. Armed with new skills, including a pilot's license, new confidence, the vision of a larger world, and the GI bill, Daddy returned to Blackwell and took up work as a crop duster.

Another drama: When Daddy was still a child, Levada, the eldest of the Myers children, had married the tall and dashing Booker McDaniel, one of three brothers from the Arkansas River valley who were something like local legends because they had reared themselves after being orphaned and, by all accounts, had done a fine job of it. Booker had become a real celebrity as a pitcher in the Negro Leagues where he played for a time with the storied Kansas City Monarchs, home team of the legendary Satchel Paige.

At some point in his career, Uncle Booker took a chance with his fortunes and joined a minor league team in Mexico. Many black American baseball players, shunned by the majors, had taken that course, finding eager audiences and starting positions south of the border. But the fast life that Uncle Booker and Aunt Levada favored took its toll after a while. They went bust. So, one day, my father, then about eighteen years old, cranked up an old, decrepit pickup truck and drove from Blackwell, Arkansas, to the Mexican border, retrieved his big sister, her dejected husband, and their belongings, and chug-a-lugged back to the town on one side of the road, thousands of miles away. Such was life in those times.

Although he was accustomed to the ups and downs of destitute life, Daddy longed for something better. And so he made a daring decision. Where most of the people in his area considered a high school diploma an arch achievement, my father wanted a college education. He certainly had the mental acumen for it. Now, with his veteran's benefits, he had the means, meager though they were. In segregated Arkansas, however, the choices for a black college prospect were few, regardless of his or her economic standing.

In the fall of 1947, Daddy took a bus to Little Rock, the capital city, and enrolled in Philander Smith College, a school run by the Methodist Church and named for its chief benefactor and founder. Philander Smith was a haven for the rare, college-bound black student, and those fortunate enough to enroll took the privilege seriously. Yearbook photographs from the late 1940s and early 1950s prove the point. Male students are typically pictured in coat and tie. Female students wore hats and gloves. Even the casual shots of students strolling the campus betray a formality and propriety unheard of today.

All through college, my father maintained two or three odd jobs at a time for spending money and cash to send home. Still, academically, he stayed at the top of his class. However, something other than textbooks, his beloved Alpha Phi Alpha fraternity, his fledgling tennis game, and Philander's Shakespearean theater group, had caught his eye. As it did for a pretty, petite, smart, and soft-spoken coed named Rachel Helms, the baby daughter of a subsistence farmer from south Arkansas.

Like most students at Philander Smith, Rachel knew hard times. Unlike the Myers family of Blackwell, however, the Helmses of Shady Grove owned lots of land, and on it they built their own houses; planted beans, corn, watermelons, and peas; kept setting hens, raised hogs, and had one or two horses for plowing. Local ponds and streams, neighboring woodlands, and the backyard dependably provided fish, rabbit, squirrel, chicken, or pork for the table. And if the large batch of siblings would not suffice, there were loads of cousins to play with down the road apiece where other relatives had built their houses.

A superb student, Rachel had dreamed of college, too, but the possibilities were faint. She was reluctant to even broach the topic with her solemn, hardworking father whom she adored. Her mother, Ida, had died after a long illness only the year before Rachel finished high school, and as the last daughter at home, she felt obligated to step into her mother's shoes as much as possible to keep the home fires burning.

But Nobel Helms, a private and introspective man, knew his daughter's longing. Moreover, he knew she deserved a different kind of future. One day, to her everlasting surprise and gratitude, he handed Rachel the money to register at Philander Smith, drove her to Little Rock, dropped her off with her one suitcase, and promised to "figure out" how to keep her in college. The next four years would indeed be touch and go, but, like her new boyfriend, Rachel excelled in school, impressing classmates and professors alike.

Mutually smitten, equally intelligent, and religiously faithful, Lloyd Myers and Rachel Helms were married on Christmas Day, 1949, in front of the crackling fireplace of my grandfather's living room in Shady Grove. They each finished Philander Smith with honors.

By the time my father went into the hospital for elective surgery that summer of 1962, Daddy and Mama had been happily married for thirteen years and had three children— me, born in 1953; Sandra, born in 1955; and Lloyd Anthony, who arrived in 1958. Since Mama was a teacher, her evenings were often filled with lesson plans and grading papers. Every now and then, she would go on a round of home visits, calling on her students and their parents in their own homes, a bygone practice. Regardless of her workload, dinner was invariably hot and hearty, the house was clean as a whistle, and our clothes were always clean and pressed. Too, she treated us regularly to music and readings and helped us with our homework when we needed it. Our parents were obviously in love with each other and enjoyed each other's company. It was a warm, safe, and loving home, an idyllic existence, notwithstanding the wolves of segregation and discrimination outside the door.

Over the years, Daddy had slowly but steadily moved up

the ranks at Blue Cross–Blue Shield, where, despite his business degree from Philander Smith, he had started in the mailroom. In 1959, he was ordained as a minister of the Baptist Church, an accomplishment that had left me at once proud of him and scared for me, since I worried that my new role as a preacher's kid would grind the good times to a halt.

It was, for the most part, unnecessary alarm. Our routines remained pretty much as they had always been: Sunday school, then worship services on Sunday mornings; Baptist Training Union one Sunday night a month; participation in the annual Easter and Christmas plays; and, when Daddy became pastor of a small church in 1960, weekly choir rehearsals.

But as preacher's kids, and especially as the pastor's kids, we were watched and scrutinized more closely than our unleashed peers. It is true what they say: "P.K.s" get more credit than they're due for the good things and more blame than they deserve for the bad. So we had to watch our steps, lest we embarrass our parents or, worse, make God angry.

I was glad to be a preacher's kid in those days after Daddy came home. Having a minister for a father felt like extra insurance. Surely God would protect one of His own agents, I hoped. Surely He would not leave such a righteous and devoted man incapacitated or dead.

In truth, Daddy's situation was grave. What we had not been told was that the surgery Daddy purportedly elected to have had turned up a cancerous tumor that had rapidly metastasized. The doctors had given him six months, maybe nine, to live. To last that long, he would have to submit to regular cobalt treatments, which made him miserably sick.

Although we did not know the facts, I became increasingly suspicious that Daddy's condition was serious. Now, the idea that God would allow my father to die made me angry.

Not the man who had come that far and defied so many odds without having compromised his goodness. Not this man of such impeccable faith and wonder that, when everyone else shuttered themselves against a thunderstorm, Daddy would sit calmly on the front porch, beholding the lightning and thunder, marveling at God's handiwork.

Not the one who cherished his wife and children, who said he would never go anywhere that he could not take his family in good conscience and never did.

Not the man who could make a sip of cold, clear water seem like a miracle made in heaven just for him.

Not the one who, every blue moon, might close the blinds, grab his wife's hand, and show us how he used to jitterbug back in his dancing days.

Not this wonderful, loyal, honest, brilliant, enchanting man.

I continued to send my urgent prayers aloft, hoping to be heard in spite of my decidedly impatient and somewhat disgusted heart.

About three weeks after Daddy's homecoming, the man in the long white doctor's coat came back to our house. This time, he met in the living room with Mama alone. I leaned against the wall to eavesdrop. I heard words like "imperative" and "only chance" and "irresponsible." Heavy words. Ominous words. I heard "not even last six months" and "please convince him." I heard my mother's voice, low and calm. I heard her say "I'm sorry" just as the man was leaving.

It was later that I learned what that conversation was about. To the surprise and consternation of his doctors, Daddy had abruptly and emphatically refused further cancer treatments. The cobalt had left him too weak and ill to enjoy what life he had left, he had told them, and that was not how he wanted to spend the remainder of his days.

The doctors had turned themselves inside out with worry and disapproval, pleading with Daddy to reconsider. Their appeal to my mother to "please convince him" had been a last-ditch effort to save him.

I still do not know what conversations transpired between my father and mother during that time. I imagine they were anguished and poignant discussions, wrapped in prayer. All I know is that Daddy was resolute, dismissing the doctors with a declaration. "I've gone this far with you," he said, "I'm going the rest of the way on God's promises." With that, and with Mama's consent, there was nothing more the doctors could do.

Indeed my father did die. But before he left, he lived well and fruitfully.

He got to know and adore John, his fourth child and second son.

He got to see his children marry.

He got to cuddle and care for seven of his eleven grandchildren, who, today, look, sound, behave, and think like him.

He got to pastor and grow a lively new church.

He got to take in many more rounds of lightning and sips of cold, clear water.

He got to plant scores of saplings and watch them tower in green.

He got to love and honor Rachel for nearly fifty years.

He got to stand in a pulpit one more time and preach a sermon.

And it was there that he took his leave on the day before Thanksgiving in 1986, twenty-four years after the doctors had delivered their dire warning; twenty-four years after he had rejected man's medicine in deference to God's cure; twenty-four years after he showed us just what God can do. It was not until then that he died. And with no sign, whatsoever, of cancer.

2

The Second Opinion

Faith healers have a long tradition in America. A good number of these men and women who claim to be God's emissaries have proven to be no more than agents of their own aggrandizement. Over and over, fake "healers" have been exposed for their shams, including prearranged "miracles" and piles of money collected as "donations" or "love offerings" from would-be healed. In those cases, about the only thing who benefited from a laying on of hands was the con man or woman's bank account.

It's different for faith *healing*. The belief that God can and will relieve or banish a disease or condition has borne fruit countless times, and the medical community, which usually consigns such cases to the mystery file, has lately begun to accredit the healing powers of faith and its animator, prayer. A flurry of studies in the 1990s found that prayer, whether by a patient or an intercessor, had salubrious effects on some patients.

For example, in October 1999, a team of doctors writing in

the *Archives of Internal Medicine,* reported a demonstrable link between "remote, intercessory prayer" and marked improvements in heart patients. The team's experiment involved nine hundred coronary patients divided into two groups: those who had people praying for them, and those who did not. The study claimed "the first names of patients in the prayer group were given to a team of outside intercessors who prayed for them daily for four weeks. Patients were unaware that they were being prayed for and the intercessors did not know and never met the patients." The researchers concluded that "remote, intercessory prayer was associated with lower CCU [cardiac care unit] course scores. This result suggests that prayer may be an effective adjunct to standard medical care."

The idea that "prayer changes things"—and, by extension, the implication that those "things" include health threats—may be news to the secular world, but it's a widely received conclusion among people of faith.

For instance, Dee McClendon of Orlando, Florida, doesn't need formal research to tell her healing can come through faith. She has her own case study.

On any given Sunday morning, Dee can normally be found at the front of the sanctuary of Mount Pleasant Baptist Church, singing and raising her hands in praise. As a member of the Praise Team, she urges fellow worshippers to join her in song and prayer at the start of morning services. But on Sunday, June 6, 2003, Dee asked the congregants to help her, announcing, "I need you all to pray for me."

As Dee explained it, she was scheduled to undergo surgery that coming Friday. She didn't give details, but some of her closest friends in the church knew what had precipitated Dee's solicitation of prayer. Doctors had discovered a lump in each of her breasts.

For as long as she can remember, Dee has made May her month for taking care of "female stuff." A thorough checkup, including Pap test and mammogram, was always part of Dee's May schedule. Invariably, the visit, and the results from the tests, were uneventful.

However, the card that arrived in her mailbox on May 19 was not congratulatory but foreboding. It informed Dee that the mammogram had indicated some "abnormalities" in her breasts. She should see her physician again.

The right lump was palpable. Both Dee and her doctor could locate it by touch. Neither could feel the left lump, but the mammogram film clearly showed a worrisome mass in that breast, too. The doctor scheduled a lumpectomy for Friday, June 11.

The uncertainty about the growths in her body and the impending medical procedure made Dee nervous. She dreaded the possibility that the lumps were cancerous and malignant. She dreaded the fact that, even with the lumpectomy, she wouldn't know her status for a while. She dreaded telling her family, especially her young daughter, whom she planned to usher into adulthood.

But Dee was a praying woman. Moreover, her own mother

had fervent faith. So the women asked God to watch Dee, to heal her and to guide the surgeon's hands. Five days before she was scheduled to go under the knife, Dee asked her church family to pray for her, too.

Friday morning arrived. "I was supposed to be at the hospital at eleven A.M., but they called and said there had been a cancellation, so could I come earlier?" Dee recalled. "So I got in there that morning and they put me in a hospital gown, put me in my room, and did all the blood work and the EKG. I signed all the papers. Then, a nurse came in to put the IV into my arm. She couldn't find a vein, so she just kept poking around there. It was really painful."

Just then, Dee's doctor and an anesthesiologist came into the room. They reviewed the procedure with her and offered assurances to the anxious patient. "I don't know how to explain it, but something just came over me and I asked the doctor, would you please just check my breasts for me one more time? Now, both breasts were already marked for surgery. There were arrows all over them. But the doctor comes over anyway and he checks my right breast—the one with the lump we could feel—and he says, 'Mrs. McClendon, where's the lump, where's the lump?' "

Perplexed and cautious, the doctor sent Dee to the hospital lab for a last-minute ultrasound on both breasts. To everyone's amazement, the breast tissue was clear. More tests followed and all were normal. Incredulous nurses and doctors took turns squeezing and pressing Dee's breasts, searching for the telltale lumps. Rushed mammogram films were viewed and reviewed. But nothing. The lumps were gone.

"The doctor told me I could go home," Dee says. "He told me, 'I cannot operate on something that's not there. So what can we do for you?' I told him, they could unhook me and let me get dressed."

Dee had one more request. "I had fasted the day before and I was pretty hungry by then, so since everybody had some unexpected free time, I suggested that we get something to eat. I asked them, what's for breakfast?" It was a happy morning.

As Dee prepared to leave the hospital, her doctor conceded he was mystified by the lumps' disappearance, but "he said he sees miracles all the time." The doctor admitted that, whatever had averted the surgery, he was relieved, since the elusive left lump posed a special challenge because it was so deeply imbedded in the breast. "I told him it may have been deep, but you know what? Nothing's too deep for God."

Dee McClendon couldn't wait to get to church that Sunday morning to tell her story to the congregation. She wanted to thank them for their prayers; moreover, she wanted to let them know the prayers had worked.

Early that morning, the phone rang in the McClendon household. It was Dee's son, Darius, a twenty-year-old whose army unit had been in Kuwait and Iraq for seven months. Throughout the military buildup in the region, the spring campaign to oust Saddam Hussein, and the edgy and often deadly aftermath of war, Dee followed developments with a mixture of pride and trepidation.

"When he called that morning, it was the first time I had

heard from him in a long time," Dee said. "I was just over-joyed."

But Darius had more than just greetings; he had news.

"Mama, I just wanted to let you know that I'm getting on a plane right now," he told her. "I'm coming home."

I can give my own testimony about what might be called "prayers of prevention."

Like Dee, my oldest child, Meredith, once faced a surgical procedure that, though common and routine, held the possibility that she might have difficulty conceiving and bearing children. It was a remote possibility, but it doesn't take much of one to frighten a young woman who dreams of holding her own baby in her arms one day.

I had tried to console Meredith with facts that showed what the odds were and, of course, with a promise to help her through it all, but as we approached the assigned day for the procedure, I could tell she was growing more and more nervous. We both prayed over it—separately and together—and waited.

The night before the procedure, Meredith developed a severe case of hives—the result, no doubt, of jangled nerves. The outbreak was so bad that Meredith was soon covered in large welts and, at one point, the swelling threatened her breathing. We rushed to the emergency room.

There, the staff administered oxygen and steroids. After about an hour, the welts began disappearing and Meredith's breathing and heart rate returned to normal. But the doctors were uneasy with the prospects of Meredith undergoing anesthesia the very next morning and recommended that we postpone the procedure. We were grateful for the reprieve, but still, the operation loomed. We prayed some more.

Then the doctor called and asked Meredith to come in for a pre-op consultation. During that visit, he checked her again. The trouble was gone. The surgery was canceled. The episode with the hives had been a blessing disguised as a curse.

Of course, some people will attribute occurrences like these to the fickleness of fate. These things happen, they'll say. It's one of those anomalies, an inexplicable event, a phenomenon that life serves up every now and then. It is difficult, maybe impossible, for them to comprehend that the Unseen Mover was on the case. In the absence of an explanation befitting science or human logic, they write off such occurrences as unsolved mysteries. Isn't it something that people will believe in mysteries but will not accept the precept that a force is behind them . . . and that the force is God?

3

———

A Cautionary Jolt

Until my father's brush with death in the early 1960s, God had been a hazy figure to me—mainly I thought of Him as a benevolent dictator, who was kind beyond belief to those who obeyed and pleased Him, but mean as all get-out to those who violated His laws. I should have known better. Neither my father's ministry nor the church we attended was of the hellfire-and-brimstone variety. To the contrary, we were barraged by testimonials and examples of God's mercy and goodness, from long, long ago and up to the minute. But as a child, I went to church because my parents made me and I worshipped God because, frankly, I was afraid not to. To tell you the truth, I got baptized so I could be a full-fledged member of our church and become a junior usher. Oh, and I wanted to partake of the Lord's Supper every first Sunday, which only the "saved" were permitted to do.

However, when my father was in the grip of death and

miraculously not only survived but fully recovered from the cancer that threatened his life, I was persuaded once and for all that God is real and that faith works and that there was more to praising God than just going to church two or three times a week because Mama and Daddy said so. Faith and faithfulness became real to me.

It has been a long time since I wondered whether God is real or merely a figment of desperate imagination or a product of the yearning to give human life more import and meaning than it may actually have. How grand, after all, to think that an all-knowing, all-powerful spirit favors us above all creatures, so much so that He has endowed us with supreme and unique gifts, so much so that He wants more than anything to bring us back "home" to heaven. But long ago, I accepted that improbable arrangement as truth. The creator Himself wants me!

My disgrace, then, is that after seeing what I saw with my own eyes, hearing what I heard with my own ears, and feeling what I felt with my own heart, I still had the audacity to doubt and flout God in ensuing years. I am sure I have a lot of company in this department, but for once, there is no comfort, no refuge, in numbers.

I am ashamed to admit that I have been a chronic and acute abuser of this divine kindness. I shudder to think of how many times and in how many ways I have taken advantage of it, my faith running hot and cold, the degree of my faith tied to my need at any given moment. I can't count the times I have taken to my knees over the years, pleading—begging— God for some particular act of grace, mercy, or forgiveness in exchange for yet another promise to be a better child for Him.

I can't count the times He came through, whether with the solution I had proposed or some other fix. And I can't count the times I would caress the blessing and walk around on air for a while afterward, grateful and sure, and inevitably slip away, back into the arms of skepticism, back into the snare of wrong-headedness and wrongdoing, back into the trap of actually believing that God not only would forgive and save me again, but that He, in fact, found my shenanigans quaint and amusing. This has been the pathetic, ludicrous rhythm of my relationship with God.

I can say, however, that I have always wanted to be consecrated. Well, not always. There was a time when I enjoyed my reputation as a rough-talking, tell-you-where-to-stick-it, smart aleck, and witty whirlwind of a person. I soothed my conscience with the idea of how nice and compassionate I can be; indeed, how I never looked for conflict—never "started" anything—and that I was not a backstabber, a gossip, or the jealous type. My first instinct was to like people and treat them with respect and kindness, offering my friendship freely and assuming the best. Given that, I was sure God considered my sins pale in comparison to my innate goodness, so I expected Him to overlook my "bad side" and keep me in His care.

It was fairly easy to maintain this delusion because, over and over, the blessings flowed, both to me and around me. I had no incentive to change my ways or my thinking, considering the evidence of God's faithfulness toward others and me regardless of whether we returned the favor.

For example, in 1982, when I was in about the fourth month of pregnancy with my third child, I developed a horrendous toothache. The pain was headquartered in my lower right jaw, but it radiated upward to my ear and temple and downward through my neck and around to the base of my skull. I fled to my new dentist in agony.

The doctor quickly pinpointed the trouble—an abscess in a molar was full of infected fluid that bulged against the tooth's nerves. After about an hour's work, the bad tooth had been treated and repaired. I was sent on my way with an antibiotic to stave off recurring infection. I was instructed to call back if I had any further trouble.

I did. The very next day, after the anesthesia had long worn off, I found myself writhing anew in pain. This time the ache was more localized—it was limited to the area around the problem molar—but it was severe and disabling. My husband made arrangements for the dentist to "work me in" to his afternoon schedule.

Upon examination, the dentist determined that the new pain was related to the several injections I had been given to anesthetize the tooth and its surroundings the day before. At least one of the shots had been administered in the small area where the upper and lower jaws conjoin. An injury there, the doctor acknowledged, is almost always transient and self-healing, but in the meantime can be excruciating. He promptly scribbled a prescription for a painkiller.

Since the pain was still on the loose, I planned to waste no time getting the prescription filled at a nearby pharmacy. But on the way there, something told me to go elsewhere.

"Take me to the pediatrician's office," I told my husband. "The pediatrician?" he said. "Why?" The man looked exasperated. No doubt he wondered whether the pain was behind this irrational decision that would only delay relief.

"I don't know," I said. "Something tells me to check this prescription first."

I had been taking my children to the Arkansas Pediatric Clinic since my firstborn was two weeks old. The doctors in the practice had seen her and her younger sister through ear infections, sore throats, asthma episodes, and rashes. In a few months, there would be another Mathis baby in their patient base. I trusted this group of doctors wholeheartedly and was especially fond of Dr. Collie, whose bedside manner was friendly, patient, and caring. He had always taken time to explain things so that I would know not only what had gone wrong and what it would take to cure the problem, but how and why.

Dr. Collie greeted me with a smile even though I had shown up unexpectedly in the middle of what was, as usual, a full slate of squirming, squealing babies and their anxious moms and dads. I quickly explained the toothache business, told him that I was, as we spoke, having serious pain, and showed him the prescription the dentist had given me.

"Oh my goodness," Dr. Collie said. "You can't take this."

He explained that the prescribed drug was known to have serious, irreversible effects on a fetus, especially in the first and second trimesters of gestation. Since I was only four months pregnant, he said, there was a high likelihood—a probability, in fact—that the drug would disrupt the normal development of my baby's neurological system, leading to mental retardation, cerebral malfunctions, and general disability. I would have to make do with a couple of acetaminophen tablets every four to six hours, he said.

That "something" that had caused me to rush to the pediatrician rather than to the pharmacist suddenly had an identity. I knew nothing about pharmacology and only a tad about biology and chemistry, so there was nothing in my intellectual storehouse to raise a red flag over the prescription I had been given by a trained doctor who had no motive other than to help his patient escape her pain. I realized immediately that my "hunch" about the prescription had come from God. He had planted the hesitation and wonder in my mind; moreover, He had given me a large enough dose to prompt an action that would save my unborn child a life of suffering and our family untold heartache and tribulation. And I don't doubt either that my ability to endure the tooth pain—why the acetaminophen tablets had provided relief when, normally, they did not work for me—and why the pain had subsided faster than predicted was God's doing, too.

Five months later, I gave birth to a bouncing baby boy, so abundantly healthy that he scored just a fraction below the perfect mark on the Apgar test, the standard used to assess a newborn's reflexes, motor skills, complexion, and vital signs. Mind and body were not only intact but also quite possibly exceptional.

Some years later—ironically, during a trip to the pediatrician's office—I rode down an elevator with my two healthy daughters and one healthy son toward a ground-level shop where I had agreed to stop for treats for the kids—a consolation prize, so to speak, for their having each taken an immunization.

As we neared the lobby, strange sounds began filling the elevator shafts. They were mournful, groaning sounds, followed by shrill screams. As we stepped out of our car, another elevator door opened, emptying a woman who was pushing a wheelchair. It held a young girl of about nine or ten. Her body was twisted and misshapen, her head lopped to one side, her eyes danced wildly in her head, her mouth was agape and saliva ran down its corners onto her little blue shirt. She moaned and screamed and then seemed to laugh. My children watched in conspicuous horror until I told them to stop staring. The mother fiddled with the little girl's hair and shifted her in the wheelchair, whispered something to her and pushed on to the parking lot.

I could not help but pity this mother and child. How hard it must be, I thought, to see your child in such a state even for a moment, let alone a lifetime. How many tears, how much hand wringing, how much anguish had it cost?

And I could not help but imagine my own child and my own self in those shoes, having remembered how close we had come to the same fate. But for the grace of God, who whispered a warning in my ear one ordinary day when I was pregnant, that mother and child's fate would have been my son's and mine. That was clear as a bell.

In writing this account, I was interrupted several times by inquiries from my son, now a young adult, wanting to share his intelligence about one issue or another. About the Roman Empire, about whether van Gogh was a contemporary of Picasso, about what had led to civil strife in Liberia, about the difference between "enormous" and "enormity," about recent climate changes, about the genius of hip-hoppers Tupac Shakur and Eminem.

He is a good son, a good-looking son, and he has been gifted with a brilliant, inquisitive mind and a tender heart. For all of his life, he has been a joy and, by turns, full of it. And there is this: He has been so easy to care for. God has watched over him since the womb, and even before that I suppose. Why he was spared deformity and incapacity is a mystery whose purpose is yet to unfold. Who knows? Maybe I would have been a lousy special needs mother.

At any rate, we are watching. We are paying attention. And we are both trying to stay close to God so His whispers won't be drowned out by our own voices.

It is hard work, staying faithful. And God forgive us for that, because we certainly cannot say He hasn't given us plenty of reason to be.

4

―

Search and Rescue

For a while there in the 1950s and 1960s, one of the hottest characters in all of pop culture was Popeye the Sailor Man—a lowbrow, low-tech version of the Everyman superhero. Like most TV idols in those days, Popeye was a good guy—loyal, sincere, and ready to defend and protect the helpless and distressed. He was at a decided disadvantage, however, when he crossed paths with that bulbous bully Bluto, who seemed to want whatever Popeye had, especially his girlfriend Olive Oyl.

But anytime Popeye had had enough of Bluto's atrocities—as signaled by those immortal words, "It's all I can stands and I can't stands no more"—viewers knew Bluto was about to get his comeuppance. A large can of spinach would appear from Popeye's sleeve or his pocket, and as he scarfed it down, his biceps would bulge, sometimes in the shape of an anvil. The spinach, we were led to believe, had transformed Popeye into a bold and muscle-bound combatant and, apparently, improved his wits as well. Invariably, Bluto would get what was coming to him in spades. Because of Popeye, a lot of kids believed spinach would give them superhuman strength.

The human beings in the cartoons were ahead of us then and still are. Try as we might—and we are certainly trying—we have yet to find a magic vegetable or potion or pill capable of converting our mushy bellies and flabby arms to brawn in an instant. Human chemistry and physiology remain stubborn and defiant. Still, it's amazing what the body can do despite its limitations and natural constraints. I've known or heard of several examples of physical achievements that border on, if not are, miracles. Nearly all have been attributed to a chemical overdrive triggered by excitement or fear. The adrenal gland usually gets the credit. I remember one of my elementary school classmates had a spurt of fame when word spread that her mother had lifted the front end of a car after it struck her little brother and pinned him and his bicycle to the pavement. That's when I first learned about adrenaline and its ability to temporarily boost strength and stamina. The adults said it accounted for the woman's burst of power.

There was probably a flood of adrenaline among the hordes of onlookers on Washington, D.C.'s Fourteenth Street bridge one January day in 1982 when an airliner plunged into the Potomac River. Its wings disabled and weighed down by ice, the plane had crashed into the crowded bridge and burrowed into the icy river with seventy-eight passengers and crew on board. The crowd grew frantic as a handful of survivors struggled in the frigid waters.

They cheered when a rescue helicopter plucked one man from the waters and deposited him safely on the riverbank. But panic struck anew when a woman who appeared to be hanging on to life by a thread lost her grip on the chopper's rescue ring and fell back into the icy deep.

Like other horrified spectators, Lenny Skutnik prayed aloud for help. But he went further. He jumped in, braving the water's paralyzing temperatures and the risk of exhaustion and injury.

"It's strange, but I didn't feel the cold," Skutnik wrote in an August 1982 essay for *Guideposts* magazine. "I didn't even hit any rocks or debris from the wreckage as I swam. I was propelled by an unexplainable strength that sent me in a straight line for the woman. I'd never taken life-saving lessons. I had no plan—none was needed. Instinctively, things just happened. I held on to her and pushed, swimming as fast as possible toward shore. I don't know how long it took. I didn't even feel tired. I don't know how to explain anything—I wasn't thinking."

Only after Skutnik was in an area hospital being treated for hypothermia did the reality of his feat dawn on him. He couldn't believe he had taken such a chance; moreover, he couldn't believe he had pulled it off. He certainly was no show-off, nor was he known for any particular athletic prowess. He hadn't been trained in rescue tactics. He wasn't even that great a swimmer. But, he remembered, his mother had taught him something about emergency response.

"She taught us to turn to God in times of trouble," he recalled in the *Guideposts* article. "I had been calling out to Him all afternoon. Could that be why He chose me? I don't know.

And I'm not at all convinced that the woman is alive today because of me. A Power greater than I took command out there in the icy Potomac."

We can honor the adrenal gland and cans of spinach if we want, but people know when it's more than that. Those who have been called by God for a particular mission and endowed with the unnatural power it takes to accomplish that mission are aware that theirs was more than just a physiological anomaly. Adrenaline, after all, doesn't bolster courage. That's a God thing. Just ask Lenny Skutnik.

5

Long, Dark Road

Lest we think there are some things too trite for God to involve Himself in, some places too low for His hand, consider Michael Walker-Jones, a Massachusetts lawyer and educator who, not once but twice, had an encounter with God's grace on the occasion of, of all things, car trouble.

The first time was in 1989 when Michael was in law school. He had a young family, only a part-timer's income, and a ten-year-old Volvo in which, one weekend, Michael, his son, and a cousin set out for a trip to a friend's house.

About twenty-five miles outside Franklin, Massachusetts, the Volvo broke down. The car was towed to a nearby mechanic who popped the hood and quickly determined that the engine was shot. Michael would need a new one.

"Now, I'm in law school and I have virtually no money and my family and I need this one car," Michael said. "I'm saying, 'Oh, goodness; how in the world am I going to get this thing fixed?'"

As usual, Michael prayed over it. He had been raised in a praying household by a great-grandmother who took Michael and his younger brother and sister into her one-bedroom home in Louisville, Kentucky, when Michael was seven. After three years of that arrangement, Michael's grandmother—the old woman's daughter—quit her job in Michigan and moved into the Louisville home to help care for the energetic young brood. With little money but considerable faith, the two women reared the children to healthy young adulthood.

"I was on semester break when the engine blew in the car," Michael recalled. "During that break, I got a call from a woman who says, 'You know, we had someone who was scheduled to do a workshop here and they just canceled. Can you be here this next weekend? We'll pay you fifteen hundred dollars to come and do this workshop.'"

"I think it was right after she made the call that I called the mechanic and said, 'How much would it cost for a new engine?' Eight hundred dollars was his price. So, the next week, not only did I have a new engine, I had money left over."

The second time was on the evening of November 6, 2001. Michael remembers the date because it was, for him, such a clear encounter with divine intervention and grace that he says he can never forget it.

While he is an official with the Massachusetts Teachers Association (MTA), the Bay State affiliate of the National Education Association, the largest teacher's union in the country, it was more as concerned citizen and school patron that Michael had taken up the cause of a local override pass—a proposal to slightly increase property taxes in order to bolster funding for Franklin's public schools. November 6 was Election Day.

In the few days prior, Michael had divided his time between work with the MTA, campaigning for the override pass, and traveling with a couple of friends who specialized in working with troubled, at-risk kids and street gangs. The trio had been conducting workshops and gatherings around the state for adults involved in gang prevention.

As Election Day broke, however, Michael bowed out of the antigang workshops. It was the final push, the last chance, to persuade voters that their tax dollars were desperately needed by and could do significant good for public education. Michael had both hope and history riding on the outcome. "Out of the fifteen times that I've done this, I had only lost one election," Michael said. "It's not been my history to work with a group to get an override and lose." But it would be a tough sell.

Michael asked his colleagues to go on to the next antigang workshop near Cape Cod. He would drive down after the polls had closed and the override issue had been decided. They could take his car and he would hook up with them later, at the hotel.

"When the results came in that night . . . we had lost the ballot question nearly three to one," Michael said. "I had arranged for a celebration party, which you always anticipate, but instead it was a wake. So we're all depressed and down and at the same time we're vowing to continue with the struggle."

Dazed, worn, and disappointed, Michael collapsed into a borrowed car for the two-hour drive to the Cape. "I didn't have the radio on or anything. It was quiet in the car." Then, suddenly, it wasn't. The car began to shimmy and shake. It made a couple of peculiar noises and slowed to a stop. It was nearly ten P.M. and Michael was on a dark road—a rarely traveled one, apparently—and out of gas. Unusually, he didn't have his cell phone; it was in the car his friends had taken earlier in the day.

"I get out of the car and realize I'm between exits. The next one is about a mile ahead of me. So there's nothing to do but start walking. Eventually, I see a filling station. But when I get there, don't you know that it had just closed about ten minutes earlier? So I kept walking down this road about another two miles. The next business that I see that's open is a liquor store. The guy inside says the only gas station that he knows of is about five miles farther down the road. And he says, 'But I'll tell you what: I have a gas can. I filled it up today for the lawn mower and I can let you have that.'"

Relieved, Michael accepted the offer and took a service road for the three-mile walk back to the car on the darkened highway.

"I'm walking and walking and thinking there's got to be a way to get back onto the highway from this service road. I go down this one road and it basically leads to a dead end. I see a field that looks like it should lead to the highway, but something tells me, no; don't go across that field. So I turn around and go back to the main service road, realizing I'm going to have to backtrack to get back onto the highway. It's going to be a long night."

Suddenly, two headlights blast into view, dispelling the darkness. It's the young man from the liquor store with his father. "He said, 'I got my wife to come in so she's running the store and my father and I are here to help you. So get in and I'll take you back to your car.'

"As he's taking me to my car, he says, 'You know what? This is very interesting because I was in Florida about a year ago and my car ran out of gas. I didn't know anybody and this guy came up to me and he helped me. So I thought I ought to help you.'"

Michael offered money to his rescuer, but the young man declined. "He says the only thing he wants me to do is to help someone else out one day. As I'm thinking about this, my heart is just leaping. I'm saying to myself, me walking in this direction, that filling station closed by ten minutes, and even my going down the wrong road, I'm there at that point and time. This guy told me that story saying that he knew he owed this debt. And here's the Lord working, giving me a chance to get myself settled and giving him the opportunity to pay off his debt. This has got to be divine providence."

Should you make the mistake of calling Michael's good fortune a stroke of luck rather than divinity, you are in for a lawyer's case to the contrary. When the car first came to a standstill, he says, he sat there stewing for ten minutes—long enough for the nearest service station to close for the night. When he finally set out, he chose the direction that took him to the liquor store where, Michael notes, the attendant just happened to have filled up a gas can that very day. Finally, had he taken the main highway rather than the service road, he would have missed meeting the man and his father.

"I knew during this whole experience that if it hadn't been for him coming, I would have never known his story. But being in the car with him and his father gave me the opportunity to meet some really kind people. The Lord wanted me to hear his story."

Despite the long and trying night, Michael arrived at the Cape in high spirits, his good cheer and hopefulness restored.

"What's a stupid election? There's always another chance," Michael said. "What I needed to be reminded of that night is that there are lots of good people in this world. You can always count on that."

PART TWO

Sanctify, Cleanse,

Renew, and Pardon

6

The Arraignment

Marsha's head throbbed from confusion and anger and fear. And from the repeated blows administered by her jailers as she lay, hog-tied, on a concrete block in the dark, cold cell. What was happening? How had it come to this?

For years, Marsha Allen had led a charmed life. Not that it had started out that way. Her life began not only inauspiciously but also hazardously. At her birth, the doctor in attendance, a resident, was somewhere in the hospital napping, having declared that her delivery was not imminent. So, Marsha's thirty-six-year-old mother, Marsielle, had to give birth to her fifth child without assistance or medical attention. "I was kind of powered out of the womb without any assistance for my mother," said Marsha. "That's where it started."

Despite that risky beginning, life was as good as it could be for a black girl in Atlantic City, New Jersey, in the 1950s. Marsha had a loving, intact family—working class but comfortable.

Marsielle even owned her own beauty shop, and many a day, little Marsha would be underfoot, busying herself with childish things, and, even as a tot, putting together the two and twos that produce the logics of life.

On one of those days at the beauty shop, Marsha remembers a woman coming in with a magazine full of hairdos. She pointed to the one she wanted replicated. But, Marsha noted, "the hairstyle required about twelve inches of hair and the woman only had about three." Marsha watched as her mother combed and brushed and pushed and swirled the woman's hair until at least the front of it resembled the magazine picture. "I remember thinking, why do they do that? Why don't they tell them they don't have enough hair? And that was my first sense that what was not was more important than what was."

In 1964, tragedy struck the Allen household. John Allen, who loved to fish, had taken his boat to nearby Brigantine, New Jersey, and had not come back. "The first day I remember saying, well, somebody came up in their boat and he got on their boat because his car was found at the dock," Marsha recalled. "I remember just coming up with all this stuff other than he's dead."

But searchers found John Allen's body on the third day after he went missing. He had drowned in the Back Bay. The sudden loss of her father sent Marsha's family into an emotional and financial tailspin. At forty-eight, Marsielle was suddenly a widow with twelve-year-old Marsha and a fifteen-year-old. After funeral expenses, the meager proceeds from John's life insurance policy didn't last long. The Allens' nice life in the bustling resort town abruptly turned to sorrow and struggle.

Already five feet seven, it wasn't hard for Marsha to pass herself off as older than her dozen years. When she popped up at a lodging house that catered to Jewish tourists and applied for a job as a chambermaid, she got it. Not that she was any good at turning sharp, crisp corners on a bed, as the owners soon realized. But rather than let her go, her new employer put her on the desk, answering phones, sorting mail and keys, and running errands for the guests.

Mrs. Allen objected to her youngest child's going to work at such a tender age, but Marsha insisted. "I'm looking at her and thinking, I know things aren't the way they used to be and you need help. There were things I wanted and I knew she wouldn't be able to get them for me and I didn't have any expectation that she should because my dad wasn't there and we needed the money." As Marsha tells it, from that day to this, she has paid her own way.

The gratification of contributing to the strained household budget and the business of adapting to the family's new circumstances, however, were interrupted, when Marsha's best friend, a girl named Regina, drowned that same summer during a trip to the beach that Marsha had decided to forgo. "I began to think that if I had been there, since I could swim, I could have helped her and it wouldn't have happened," she said sorrowfully. Over the next handful of years, she would lose two other close pals to the Atlantic—her first boyfriend, Bobby, who drowned in the bay, and another good friend, Peter. Marsha says the serial tragedies took a toll on her emotions. Early in her teenage years, she said, she learned to freeze her feelings.

Nevertheless, Marsha was occasionally buoyed by pride

and joy, especially during her high school years when her life, riddled by sorrow and loss, began to swing decidedly upward. She had always been an exceptional student and more than a few adults in her world had taken notice. Marsha wanted to go to Howard, the historic black university in Washington, D.C., and alma mater to many of the country's most prominent black lawyers, doctors, and educators. But just in case Howard had no scholarship for her, and she would need one because of the family finances, Marsha had a backup plan: She would also apply to Atlantic City Community College—a respectable two-year institution but unlikely to present the challenge a brain like Marsha's deserved.

"A Jewish woman named Joyce Anderson had taken an interest in me," Marsha explained. "She said I should apply to her alma mater, which she said was an Ivy League school. I'm like, 'What's an Ivy League school?' It was amazing what I didn't know then." Mrs. Anderson had graduated years before from the University of Pennsylvania and thought Marsha would make a good fellow alumna. She wrote a letter of recommendation for Marsha, who duly applied to Pennsylvania, Howard, and the community college. She was accepted at all three, but only the University of Pennsylvania had the financial assistance she needed—a package that included a $16,000 scholarship, student loans, and work-study grants. So Pennsylvania it was.

Marsha worked even harder the summer between high school graduation and her freshman year at Penn, hoping to buy a few new clothes and odds and ends for her dorm room in college. Then, out of the blue, she received a call from the director of her high school band, which Marsha had led as drum majorette. The Atlantic City High School band was preparing to lead the 1970 Miss America Pageant parade per tradition. But since Marsha had just graduated, the band no longer had anyone with the skill and experience to lead the band in such a high-profile and prestigious engagement. Would she pull on her boots this one last time?

A veteran overachiever and habitual workaholic, Marsha agreed to don her boots and uniform, to strut the mace, and to wear the towering majorette's hat for the ritual that marked the opening of Atlantic City's premiere annual event. Thousands flocked to the seaside city when the young women deemed the most beautiful and talented in all the nation came to vie for the Miss America crown and its attendant perks—the money, the scholarships, the exposure, the celebrity. The parade ignited days of festivity, glamour, and excitement in a town whose residents usually carried on their workaday lives on the periphery of good times. The long line of marching bands and beauty-laden floats would begin at the top of the boardwalk, traverse the judge's reviewing stands at Convention Hall, and not stop until it reached the high school at the opposite end.

Although Marsha had expended much of her energy and excitement on the prospect of college, the anxiety she felt over her commitment to the band director quickly turned to happy anticipation. But on parade day a problem arose. One of the heels on her old marching boots had broken. Plus, that was the day she had to register for classes at the University of Pennsylvania. "I had to get up early in the morning and go to college and register in Philadelphia," she said. "And I had to run around and get a new pair of boots, which is not a great thing, marching seven miles in new boots."

By the time Marsha reported for the parade lineup, her stomach was nervous. And empty. In all of her running around, she had not had time to eat. "My dear mother was worried because she knew I had gotten up at five in the morning to register in Philly, bought books, came back to Atlantic City, and reported for the lineup without anything to eat."

Youth and adrenaline propelled Marsha forward. "I'm on national TV leading the band. At this point, I'm six feet tall and my headdress is like two feet. And then there are the boots—those new boots squeezing my feet—so I'm about nine feet tall. And I had my mace and there I go. There was a part of me that was frozen and this other part that just went for it. I would come down that boardwalk and it was time to entertain and I was going to step. You could imagine—this was Boogaloo time. I did it—in good taste, but, hey, let's do it."

Two miles down the boardwalk, Marsha happened to look to one side of the walk with its thick crowds, waving and cheering and applauding. Suddenly, Marsha spotted her mother. "She's worried I'm going to pass out, so she's got a bottle of water and some food. She was fifty-four years old and do you know that she marched with me all the way to the end of the bridge? I tell you that until I got to Jesus, her love sustained me in this world." Marsha capped off the summer by winning first runner-up in the Miss Black Pennsylvania contest.

● ● ●

It would be some time before Marsha came to know what God could, and would, do. Her mother had instilled in her a vague notion of God. She believed there was a divine power, but, as she says, she did not have an understanding of how He worked or, for that matter, what He wanted from her. Yet she called on this hazy power from time to time as she labored through the transition to college life. For example, at the University of Pennsylvania, there were some painful run-ins with racial prejudice. Right after she checked into her freshman dorm, her Chinese roommate showed up, took one look at Marsha, said hello, and left the room never to be seen again. Marsha says it was God who showed her the silver lining in that cloud; she relished having a large room to herself.

Overall, Marsha prospered at the university, impressing her professors with her diligent, agile, and strong mind, her engaging wit, and a work ethic that put other students to shame. Her social life and popularity thrived too, thanks to Marsha's effervescence, good mind, and good looks. In her senior year, Marsha was again first runner-up in the Miss Black Pennsylvania contest.

As an urban studies major, Marsha believed she found her calling when, in her third year at Pennsylvania, she took an internship with the chief economic planner to the mayor of Newark, New Jersey. In the field, she saw a devastating sight. "When I saw downtown Newark and the neighborhoods with people pooping in their houses and they had boards up against their windows and they didn't have food, I was paralyzed," she says. So much so that the scenes of extreme poverty in the Land of Plenty haunted her in her sleep. So much so that Marsha couldn't help talking about it to her part-time employer, a wealthy, brilliant Mormon who had been blinded in a laboratory experiment years before. Marsha's job was to read for the man—books, periodicals, magazines, newspapers, annual reports, studies, and executive summaries, "highbrow material" as Marsha put it.

"I was really in tears," Marsha recalls. "I said, 'You know these men downtown with all these briefcases and suits that all look the same and they have these trench coats—Burberry, Hickey Freeman? What is it that they know?' And he said, 'Businesspeople know how to fix things.' Now, I was a child of the seventies, and I didn't want to be a part of the world of big business. But I was brought to my knees. How could they be so poor in one place in the same town? And my employer said, 'Well, if you want to make a difference, you have to know what the businesspeople know. Doesn't mean you have to be like them, but you have to know what they know.' So now, this is a complete change for me, majoring in city planning, to now talk about business. I hadn't even taken a business course."

Although Marsha had planned to pursue a master's degree in public administration after college, that conversation changed her mind. Her employer encouraged her to go after a master's of business administration. He had one from Wharton and it had secured his own comfortable station. And it had put him in the network of movers and shakers. If Marsha wanted to change things, an MBA was the ticket, he said.

In the spring of 1974, Marsha took her bachelor of arts degree in urban studies with honors. That fall, she enrolled in the venerable Harvard Business School, which had not hesitated to accept her into its exclusive program.

Marsha thrived in the heady atmosphere at Cambridge. Networking came naturally to her and, in short order, she joined the school's Marketing Club, Finance Club, and the Public Affairs Forum. She was a section editor of the yearbook and a member of the Harvard/Radcliffe Cultural Center board. She received a coveted Council of Graduate Management Education (COGME) fellowship and the *Wall Street Journal's* prestigious Student Achievement Award. At the same time, she worked in the Business School's admissions office.

With two Ivy League degrees, Marsha waltzed through the business world, building a power base and a golden résumé at a series of Fortune 500 giants—first IBM, then AT&T, and, in 1982, at The Equitable Life Assurance Society for the United States.

With her executive perks and big-league salary and no husband or children to care for, Marsha enjoyed the good life. She owned her own home, drove a Mercedes-Benz, employed housekeepers and gardeners, dressed to the nines, and traveled as she pleased. Statuesque, pretty, smart, and well-to-do, Marsha had her share of suitors, too. She was drawn to three men especially. Marsha would allow "a block of time" to pass in switching from one lover to the next "because I couldn't sleep with them both at the same time." That is what passed for good conscience then, she says.

But the danger and ignominy was compounded by the fact that two of Marsha's partners were married. Those relationships, though full of intrigue and passion at the time, would later bring disaster.

In 1982, Marsha put an end to the carousing and married her on-again, off-again boyfriend, another Harvard Business School graduate and fellow Fortune 500 executive, whom we will call Mr. C. When she told one of the married lovers—we'll call him Mr. A—about her betrothal, he sank into depression, having just divorced his wife so that he and Marsha could be married. Mr. A's reaction so startled Marsha that, at first, she changed her mind and told him she would become his wife. Then Marsha changed her mind again. "When I said I would go back to [Mr. C], he said I could never talk to [Mr. A] again— not ever. That was the condition of our being back together. Meanwhile, [Mr. A] said, 'You've got two years to come back to me. If you don't come back, I'm going to get married.' He was serious."

They honeymooned on Paradise Island in the Bahamas— "pink sand, clear water, gambling, money, money, money," she says. The trip was a wedding present from one of Marsha and Mr. C's Harvard classmates. The first two days were blissful for Marsha and Mr. C. They lounged at the water's edge, made love, shopped, visited the casinos, and danced through the night. On the third day, the newlyweds went sightseeing and, crossing a bridge, came upon a scene that would disturb Marsha's happy-go-lucky heart.

"I saw the tourists throwing money into the ocean," she recalls. "And these little street urchins were diving in and getting the money and being clownish and entertaining. And it takes me back to the memory of when I was going to the boardwalk and I'm about eight and the firemen had an event. They had a band and I started dancing and people on the boardwalk started throwing money down. I'm really dancing now. I went home and showed my money to my mother. She said, 'Where did you get this?' I told her and she whipped my butt. So that flashback came to me when I saw those children clowning for money. Then I went into the town and saw those shanties. That was the end of my honeymoon."

Over her new husband's protests, Marsha went to work. She asked the concierge for fifty of the little notepads that hotels place on the bedside tables in the guest rooms. She grabbed a towel and marched out to the swimming pool. "And for the next four days, I sat by the pool and wrote 'One Life to Live: A Journey into the Technology of Producer Results.' I wrote a twelve-week course. I said, 'I'm going to help the people who don't know how to play this game. I'm going to teach them the things I learned from being around these people and I'm going to break it down.'"

That was in June of 1982. By that December, she had convened her first class of sixteen people—all friends and acquaintances who each agreed to pay $500 for the twelve-week course. As a show of good faith and her earnest intentions, Marsha allowed each enrollee to write his or her own payment plan. She would accept $10 a week, the full $500 at the end of the class, whatever the students chose. "The principle I was promoting was you need to give your word and you need to keep it and you need to think through what you will have to do to keep it. I found that if you operated based on this principle, you would accomplish your goal."

To show that she meant it, Marsha's first act as instructor was to announce that she was giving up cigarettes. "All of the people knew I was a smoker and that I didn't really like the habit. I wanted to convey to them how people could live this one life and be successful. And so I said I would declare something I wanted to do and I would organize my resources around it. So I said, 'I declare that I will quit smoking today forever and I will never take one puff.' Everybody was, like, 'wow,' because they knew how I felt about not being able to stop this habit. For me to declare myself had to mean that I was willing to go up against all of these forces that were keeping me down."

The classes were a hit and word spread quickly about the successful businesswoman and her twenty-six principles for success. More than half of that first class signed on for special training as instructors, demand for classes increased, and, soon, Marsha's program had to be expanded from one class a week to three, with thirty students in each class. Within two years, One Life to Live had an enrollment of two hundred fifty.

Marsha's mind went into overdrive. It was time to take her success plan to the next level. So she developed a new curriculum, the Entrepreneurial System of Living "for people who didn't want to be boxed into the system." And Marsha practiced what she preached. Her success with the twelve-week courses had seeded a whole range of interests now under the umbrella of MAC Enterprises, Inc., which she founded in 1984. The corporation included the seminars, nine profit centers in five cities, a health retreat, a boutique, management consulting, and the development of a time management calendar system for retailers. That same year, Marsha's soft smile graced the cover of *Savvy* magazine, which hailed her as a woman on the move.

Then the crash began.

Upon her marriage to Mr. C, Marsha had left AT&T—partly to get away from her old liaisons and get a fresh start—and taken a job as vice president with The Equitable. She and her husband had left New York and moved to neighboring New Jersey where they bought a house. Per usual for top-drawer executives, Marsha got a generous relocation package from The Equitable and she used part of the funds to repay herself for the money she had already advanced to her husband for the down payment on the New Jersey house Mr. C had been determined to buy. She did not claim expenses for the apartment she had leased and was living in alone since, already, the relationship was in trouble.

The paperwork on the mortgage transaction raised a red flag. "They called me in and said, 'You owned the house already and you used these relocation benefits,' " Marsha remembers. "I said to them, 'No, that's not what happened.' My shame over my personal relationships caused me to only tell what happened at the level of the transactions, not that I had my own apartment. So I was trying to explain that it wasn't what it appeared to be but it would only make sense if I told the whole thing to them and I wasn't willing to do that."

Frustrated and stunned by the innuendo, Marsha apologized to The Equitable, agreeing to repay the entire relocation package plus interest, tens of thousands of dollars. She also agreed to relinquish her corporate perch. Shortly, Marsha resigned, shook hands with the company president, and stepped down from the career ladder she had so gingerly climbed. Unemployed but still ambitious, Marsha plunged into her work with MAC Enterprises and set about rebuilding her disheveled life and reinventing herself. By 1986, she had recouped both profits and acclaim. That year the New Jersey Black Legislative Group named her Entrepreneur of the Year and the Urban Bankers chose Marsha as Businessperson of the Year for her work toward revitalizing Newark and Atlantic City and in boosting the black business community.

No one knows for sure just how Marsha Allen's remade success came unraveled then, but she suspects that old colleagues in the corporate towers she had abandoned were behind the Urban Bankers' sudden decision to rescind the Businessperson of the Year award. It came down like this: Marsha got a call one day from a woman with the Urban Bankers, asking about her past problems with The Equitable. Despite Marsha's explanations— that it was a misunderstanding, that she had resigned voluntarily, that she had paid back the money, that it all happened two years prior—the woman asked Marsha to withdraw as Businessperson of the Year. Marsha refused. The Urban Bankers sent out a flurry of letters announcing that no award would be given that year.

"The day I would have received the award, I was indicted, charged with fraud. All hell broke loose. It was terrible, terrible, terrible. In the end, it was my family that stood with me and even with my husband, it came undone."

The first trial ended in a mistrial. The prosecutor pressed on. Marsha's attorney was Ramsey Clark, a rainmaker who had been attorney general in Lyndon Johnson's administration and, by dint of that experience, was one of the most powerful lawyers in the country. Before the second trial convened, however, Clark had taken on the case of Palestinian defendants in a lawsuit brought by the family of Leon Klinghoffer, a New York Jew who, in October 1985, was celebrating his wedding anniversary with wife Marilyn when PLO terrorists hijacked their cruise ship, the *Achille Lauro*. Sparking worldwide outrage, the hijackers had shot the sixty-nine-year-old Klinghoffer, who was disabled, and then dumped him and his wheelchair into the Mediterranean.

In his absence, Clark had arranged for an associate to handle Marsha's case, but the proposition failed. Marsha then hired another prominent lawyer, O. T. Wells, famous for his defense of Black Panther H. Rap Brown.

Almost from the start, Marsha and Wells did not get along. Their animosity—mutual, she says—was premised on mistrust and bad chemistry. She complained to the judge, but says her grievances were brushed aside. Eventually, the relationship with Wells turned so sour that, in one court appearance, Marsha accused the judge, the prosecutor, and Wells of collusion, declaring that "they need to start a law firm because you all are working together." The frantic scene in the courtroom left Marsha's mother distraught. Marsielle Allen fainted and had to be rushed by ambulance to a New York hospital. The diagnosis was a TIA—transient ischemic attack—a neurological disturbance brought on by a shortage of blood to the brain. Similar to stroke, TIA can cause dizziness, hearing loss, numbness, and fainting spells. Some people call them "mini strokes."

Hospital officials wanted to keep Marsielle Allen for a few days of observation and care but neither she nor Marsha was at ease there. Marsha arranged for her mother to be transferred to a hospital back home in New Jersey.

With her mother stabilized, Marsha returned to court for trial. But O. T. Wells was nowhere to be seen. It took a private phone call to the judge in his chambers to resolve the mystery of Wells's whereabouts. Marsha's lawyer had been injured, the judge told the courtroom. Someone had attacked him with a baseball bat wrapped in Christmas paper and had broken his femur. The judge had no choice but to once again declare a mistrial. Once again, the prosecutor vowed to retry the case.

For the third trial, Marsha had a third attorney—C. Vernon Mason, a well-known civil rights attorney and activist. Mason would later have his own brush with notoriety when, in 1998, he was found guilty of defaming Steven Pagones, the former Dutchess County, New York, prosecutor, in connection with the sensational case of Tawana Brawley. In 1987, when she was fifteen, Brawley suddenly burst onto the public stage with a terrifying story of having been raped and tortured by six white men in a New York park. Brawley's shocking account raised racial tensions in the city to the boiling point. Street activist Al Sharpton was soon at Brawley's side, guiding her through the media storm that ensued. Mason was there, too. One year later, a jury concluded that Brawley's story had been a hoax. In a $395 million suit, Pagones went after Sharpton and Mason for implicating him as one of Brawley's supposed assailants.

Marsha had hired Mason because of his reputation as a smart, trenchant, and daring lawyer who knew the nooks of the New York legal community. She put the case in his hands and, awaiting the next move, underwent knee surgery, taking her recovery at the health retreat she owned in the Catskills. That's where she was when the cops came to arrest her. Marsha was abruptly handcuffed and shoved into a police car bound for New York City, cast, crutches, and all.

"I'm angry now," she says. "I'm like, what is it now? Why am I under arrest now?" When she got to court, she learned she had been indicted for ordering a hit on O. T. Wells. Mason had not notified her because, unbeknownst to her, he was no longer her attorney. As a former partner of Wells's, Mason had recused himself from the case.

"Girl, if you could see the articles they wrote about that hit," Marsha told me. "There must have been about a hundred articles. *The Charlie Rose Show* called. I was on Page Six of the *New York Post*. The *New York Times* ran an article. Every major paper had something. 'Businesswoman nabbed in bat attack,' 'New definition of attorney-client privilege.' It just captured the public's attention."

This time, Marsha was jailed at Riker's Island. Bail was set at an astounding $1 million.

"When they arrested me, I had a $10,000 fur coat on. I was in the bullpen for three days because it takes that long to process you into a cell. So there I was in jail. Never been in jail in my life. I took my fur coat and put the lining on the floor and spread it out and laid down on it and went to sleep. When I woke up the next morning, there were two other people on the coat with me."

Despite the frightful, degrading details, Marsha chuckles as she recalls this. "You can have certain experiences that will really reduce your importance quickly and what is important to you. My Italian coat with female pelts. It's the only thing I've kept from that time. And I keep it for what it represents as my old life and because it was with me in my transition. Because there we were, me and two homies, in Riker's Island, asleep."

Deliverance was coming, but not yet. Marsha was beginning to recognize at least the outlines, the profiles, of the competing forces in her life—God's way versus the other way. She couldn't help but notice, for example, how desperate some people were. Like other prisoners who had been locked up for a year because no one would pay their $150 bails. "If you thought I was a problem at age three, when I noticed the lies about a woman's hairstyle, by the time they had put me in Riker's Island, they were creating their own worst enemy because my mind was dissecting the very core of how they had reduced God's creation to produce a recidivism cycle to maintain a business that started with slavery. Chain gangs meant free labor. I'm thinking, 'This is the modern version of an economic system that slavery abolished.' So now I've got time on my hands, I started studying their system."

Nearly a month passed before Marsha made bail and was released from Riker's. But there would be more time behind bars. She was convicted in The Equitable case but the judge delayed sentencing until after Marsha was tried for the assault on O. T. Wells.

In that trial, a witness testified that Marsha had told him she originally intended to put a hit on the judge, the prosecutor, and Wells but had changed her mind because "if I put the hit on all three, they would never stop looking for who did it." According to the witness, Marsha had told him, face-to-face, that she had decided to order a hit on Wells only—not to kill him, but just to "break his f-ing leg."

That witness was Marsha's own ex-husband, Mr. C. Their postmarital relationship had been rocked by property disputes and bad blood over The Equitable transactions. Marsha was not surprised to see him on the stand as a witness for the state, but it crushed her.

Her worsening financial straits dimmed Marsha's prospects of a vigorous defense. High-priced attorneys' fees and an expensive jail bond had nearly drained her resources. Accustomed to shelling out $25,000 up front, this time she had to settle for an attorney who would defend her on the assault trial for a comparatively paltry $2,000 retainer.

Marsha's main line of defense was that she had nothing to do with what happened to Wells, had never discussed any such thing with her ex-husband or anyone else, and that, indeed, on the night Mr. C alleged that Marsha was telling him about the wicked plan, she was at her mother's bedside in the Atlantic City hospital. Her mother attested to Marsha's whereabouts on the evening in question but her lawyer had not bothered to get hospital records or other witnesses to buttress Mrs. Allen's testimony. "If we had had the records, I would have been acquitted," Marsha said firmly. Instead, the jury deadlocked with nine jurors voting to acquit and three to convict. The judge called a mistrial.

By now, the house, the Mercedes-Benz, the investment properties, the money market and savings accounts—the high life—were all gone. Brilliant, successful, go-getter Marsha Allen had a conviction on her record, a sentence in limbo, another trial to endure, and she was broke. Desperately, she went back to a lawyer with whom she had had an affair, hoping to trade on their relationship for a suitable defense.

"This time, the attorney does exactly what I tell him to do," says Marsha. "The jury comes back with acquittal. Everybody is mad in the prosecutor's office because this is like egg on their face. I've still got the tape of the district attorney's press conference about me and with O. T. Wells and Mason being interviewed and the shots of them walking down the street where Wells was hit with the bat."

As arranged, Marsha's sentencing in The Equitable case soon followed. The judge gave her one year. Marsha's lawyer told her he would file a notice of appeal—a pledge that, as Marsha would later learn, went unmet.

Believing her appeal was in the works and that she was free pending the higher court's decision, Marsha longed to put some distance between herself and her past. She was convinced that a series of bad decisions and soured relations had gotten her in this mess and she wanted to get away. Marsha made plans to leave the area. The career, the material goods, the accolades, and awards? Good riddance. All she wanted now was peace. That, she knew, would mean making amends with God. "I just looked at myself and I told myself the truth and told God the truth. When I was backed into a corner, my schemes, my connivances, my manipulation to try to get out of trouble, using my own strategies rather than submitting to God—just going from the womb all the way up to that age—I just presented it to the Lord and asked Him to forgive me, to teach me a new way and teach me new speech." Renewed and resolved, Marsha moved to Mississippi.

• • •

There is a popular gospel song titled "He Knows How Much You Can Bear." The first verse of the song says "We are our heavenly father's children / And we all know that He loves us one and all / Yet there are times when we find we answer / another voice and call / If we are willing He will teach us / His voice only to obey no matter where / For He knows, yes He knows / just how much we can bear."

Marsha Allen, who had already borne much, would have more to bear. More than her hazardous birth with her mother, alone in the labor room. More than the loss of her father and various friends during her childhood, all to the Atlantic's cold, dark deep. More than the heartbreak of poverty in the midst of prosperity. More than a series of messy, dangerous liaisons. More than a decayed marriage and betrayal by the man to whom she had pledged her devotion. More than the humiliation and potential loss of freedom because of a fraud conviction and sentence. More than a charge and trial for criminal assault. More than the demise of her reputation. More than the light going out on her future. More than the loss of everything she had spent her adult life building.

Marsha was in the bathroom of her Mississippi home the day she neared the breaking point. Suddenly, the bathroom door came crashing down, knocking Marsha to the floor, leaving her twisted and wrenched on the tiles. It was the FBI, coming to arrest Marsha on a warrant issued by the State of New York. Pain seared through Marsha's body, cradling in her back. She couldn't get up. She couldn't walk. The agents first took Marsha to a hospital. And then to jail in Canton, Mississippi.

"They left me in a room and put the air-conditioning down

to sixty. I literally could not get off the floor because of my back injury, so I was going to the bathroom on the floor. My hair was matted. I was lying in my own waste. Finally, a woman from my church insisted that someone come and see about me. An attorney came and he took pictures. They ran the pictures in the local newspaper. Then they took me out of solitary confinement, I got cleaned up, and they took me to a doctor who said it sounded like I had a herniated disk in my back."

Confused, aching, and frightened, Marsha was finally allowed to call her family in New Jersey. Through local contacts, the family got in touch with Dick Gregory, the comedian and activist, who cautioned Marsha not to eat the food or take any medicine, but to "tough it out" and fast. She took Gregory's advice. In defiance of her own body's demands, Marsha refused food and medication for forty days, taking only fluids. Thanks in part to Gregory's connections, Marsha's case became something of a *cause célèbre*. Ramsey Clark rushed to her aid. So did the wiry-haired William Kuntsler, famed for defending the Chicago Seven among others. The men insisted that jail officials provide medical care for their client-friend.

"The marshals come in one night and yell, 'Allen, we're taking you to the doctor.' So, I get up and take a shower. Then I ask somebody if they know what time it is and they tell me it's three o'clock in the morning. And I start thinking, 'Who goes to the doctor at three o'clock in the morning? And I'm in Mississippi? I'm not going with them.' "

As Marsha tells it, she got out of the shower and lay back down on her cot to think. But the marshals had other plans.

She said they entered the cell, dragged her out of bed, roughly wrapped her in a sheet, mainly around her neck, snapped her picture, threw her into the backseat of a car, and headed for New Orleans, a three-hour drive away.

Marsha will never forget that trip. "We get to the airport in New Orleans and there's this big plane. It's used to transport prisoners in the federal system. All of these men are around the plane with this big shotgun. There I am, naked with just the sheet on me. I'm screaming and crying now. I don't know where they're taking me, what they're doing. I'm hysterical. The head marshal sees I don't have any clothes on me and he says, 'I'm not taking her, no way. It's all these men on board and you don't have any clothes for her.' So everyone runs around to try to find jumpsuits from some of the maintenance workers, but the head marshal still refuses to take me because of my condition."

For two hours, Marsha watched the surreal, nightmarish scene unfold from the backseat of the transport car. Now a private plane had been chartered, replete with a male nurse, a female marshal, a male marshal, and two pilots. When the marshals at last returned to the car to retrieve her, they were incensed that Marsha, frantic and hysterical, had used the sheet to tie herself into the car.

As Marsha tells the story, one marshal grabbed her by her hair to extract her from the car. Marsha punched the man in the face. "So they cut me out of the car. Now the sheet is ripped off of me. I'm stark naked at the airport and they're dragging me—handcuffed, shackled around the waist and feet. They lead me up the steps to the little plane and when I get to the top,

I'm able to kick on one side of the door and everybody falls down the steps. Now they're really mad. They hook me in the seat and I fly from New Orleans to Newark stark naked." Upon landing in New Jersey, Marsha was greeted by a cadre of law enforcement officials who had apparently been briefed on what happened in Canton and in New Orleans. Or at least the marshals' version of it. "Two marshals put a hospital-type gown on me and said if I hit them, they would hit me back. Someone has radioed ahead and said I have supernatural strength and that I ripped all my clothes off."

As Marsha was to learn, the worst was yet to come. She was repeatedly abused in the Union County Jail in Elizabeth, New Jersey. Marsha tells a horrid story of being slapped and taunted while in a wheelchair, situated in a shower beneath a cascade of icy cold water, and, finally, thrown into solitary confinement.

"There were like thirteen guards that came in the room and knocked me down, kicked me, punched me, they just beat me silly. Then they took me upstairs. They put a rubber helmet on me and put me on a concrete block and they hog-tied me— you know, my arms were shackled behind me, my ankles were shackled, and then the arms and ankles were shackled together. They beat me on my head with the rubber helmet, just blow after blow. There were blacks and Hispanics watching. They wouldn't do it, but they watched.

"Then a nurse came in and said, 'We're going to give you something to calm you down.' But I wouldn't take it because I remembered what Dick Gregory told me. Instead I took it in my mouth and held it under my tongue. When they saw that, they beat me some more and made me swallow the pill. For about three to four hours, I was paralyzed; all I could do was groan and moan."

Alone, shackled, and in pain, Marsha began to hyperventilate. "Only a little portion of my face was exposed through this little helmet," she said. "I couldn't breathe. Because I was so anxious and because of the drug they forced me to take, I knew that I would die if I didn't get control of my mind because I was losing it. I could feel my shoulder ripping because my body was off balance. I could feel the circulation leaving my hands and my ankles. It was like I was being murdered. Any movement I tried to get more comfortable, I would feel a tear. It was an impossible circumstance. I said, 'God, why?' And when I said that, a peace just came over me and I calmed down in my soul."

Marsha says that after several torturous hours, she was untied and officials informed her that she was being transferred to a facility for the criminally insane in Lexington, Kentucky, for thirty days of observation. Once there, she was assigned to an area whose occupants included a woman who had cut a baby from another woman's womb, a woman who routinely threw feces at passersby and ward mates, a woman who constantly stripped off her clothes, and a woman nicknamed the "ballerina killer" because she had molested young girls and cut off their feet for trophies.

When Marsha began talking about Ramsey Clark and Dick Gregory and William Kuntsler, about Harvard Business School and IBM and AT&T, authorities were incredulous. "They thought, 'She's really nuts,'" Marsha recalled. "So I gave them Ramsey's phone number. They actually did call him and Ramsey tells them, 'If she's crazy, she's crazy like a fox.' Now, Lexington is upset because they realize something really did happen like I said and they were being used under the guise that I had a mental problem. They wrote up a report saying I was fit to stand trial and chartered a private plane to get me out of there."

The federal prosecutor in Newark had set the last, terrible episode in motion. While Marsha was in Mississippi, she had been indicted on a criminal complaint involving a 1985 bank loan for Innovative Results, a job training and community revitalization company she had founded and for which her then-husband served as chief financial officer. The new charges meant yet another courtroom before yet another judge. The indictment, returned while Marsha was confined in Lexington, contained six charges.

Before trial, the judge offered to release Marsha on her own recognizance but she stunned the court by turning down the offer. "I got up and I told the judge, 'No, I'm not signing any papers.' I said, 'You all in this system have been harassing me since 1986 and I'm not leaving until everyone understands that you are never to bother me again.' The judge asks my attorney to talk to me, but I said, 'No, I'm not leaving. I'm staying because the work I was doing, you disrupted that. I'm staying because I need to establish what you all have done. There's nothing more important than this because if you can come and get me anytime you want, I'm staying and we're going to fight this out.'" Not even Clark and Kuntsler could persuade her to change her mind. Both powerhouses offered to take her case if she would sign herself out of custody, but Marsha again refused, insisting, "There's nothing for me to go back to, so I'll stay right here until we get this straight."

She put her stubbornness to work in her defense. After some frustrating delays, she tracked down copies of the pictures taken of her bruises and swelling in the Mississippi jail after the raid on her home. She got the court to appoint a physician to examine her injuries and to diagnose her ongoing medical problems. He prescribed air casts for her ankles and special surgical shoes to help relieve the persistent pain and crippling that wracked her body. That same physician would tell the court that Marsha's physical condition was consistent with her version of what had happened in the Mississippi and New Jersey jails.

The jury found her not guilty of one charge but convicted her of the remaining five. Marsha faced up to eighteen years in prison and $1.5 million in fines.

By this time, Marsha believed that no one could present her case better than she. She dismissed her attorney and, in a daring and risky move, won court approval to serve as her own attorney at the upcoming sentencing hearing. A court-appointed lawyer would assist.

"I got up and just broke it down to the judge that, if I was the jury, I would have convicted me too based on what they knew and what they saw," she says forthrightly. "But I told him I wanted them to understand that I was a guerrilla of grace." Recalling that day, Marsha steps back into her past and reenacts her soliloquy before the court, her words strong and unfaltering, her proud face forward.

You have people swear on the Bible when the Bible says no man swears, only God alone swears. You put up the Bible and you bring out doctrines of men to adjudicate the affairs of God's creation. So this system is not a system that can judge me. You may not understand this, but I've come to a place where you have the book, you can throw it at me. You can sentence me where I don't see the light of day for twenty years. But I'm going to say this: You throw the book because the grace of the Lord is with me. I won't apologize to this court, but I will apologize to the Lord for allowing myself to be a part of this system. And Your Honor, in a strange way, I thank you all for what you have put me through because even though it was not justice, it put me in a situation where I had no choice but to come to God and beg His forgiveness and feel His grace.

Marsha had spoken her peace. She had come clean with the judge. She had accepted responsibility for what she had done wrong. She had put all of her stock in God, confident that whatever came of her fate, He would make it all right.

The judge, seemingly moved by the odd but bold appeals—and perhaps suspicious of the circumstances of her arrest and detainment—pronounced a sentence that affirmed Marsha's resoluteness. For her conviction on the five counts, Marsha was sentenced to time served—the fourteen months she had already spent in confinement. Nor would she have to go to prison for the Equitable conviction.

• • •

Judging from news accounts of the day, authorities had a different take on what happened to Marsha Allen Collins. U.S. marshals denied having manhandled or otherwise mistreated Marsha while in their custody. And prosecutors in the final trial portrayed Marsha as more vixen than victim—a brilliant but crooked woman who used civic causes as a borrow pit for her own lavish lifestyle. In what one Atlantic City newspaper described as "a scorching closing argument," an assistant U.S. attorney described Marsha as "underhanded, slippery, slimy, conniving, and whatever other pejoratives you can use." And the judge in the case lamented that Marsha's predicament was all her own doing. She "had a chance to make a real difference and she blew it," he said.

Free at last from a worsening nightmare that had haunted her in fits and starts for nearly a decade, Marsha committed her considerable talents entirely to spiritual work. As spiritual developer for the California-based Jesus Commission Ministries, Inc., she devoted herself to evangelism and missionary work, foraging three states for lost souls.

But even the "new" Marsha found it hard to let go of every old habit. "I still had not come out of the body sins," she explained. "I got out of jail in May 1993. But it took me until 1997 to overcome that habitual sin that got me in trouble with men." Marsha believed some of the people she had crossed and implicated during the long court battles might be out to get her, so she shielded herself with a man who promised to help protect her. Though she had been celibate for several years, Marsha got sexually involved with him notwithstanding her better judgment. During that fling, she contracted chicken pox and had to be quarantined. "I almost died from it because I was forty-one. I had fever and I was hallucinating," she remembers.

Next, Marsha capitulated to, of all people, her married pastor. He gave the illicit affair a holy spin, maintaining that he and Marsha were on a divine mission together and that their relationship, if not heaven-sent, was at least approved by God. But Marsha knew better when, suddenly, her back seized and she was essentially paralyzed, taking refuge on the floor for six months.

"That's when I finally got it about sin," she says. "I was just overwhelmed about how hard it is for a human being to see holiness. Once I saw it, I was mortified. It was so clear, the root of my sin and my yoking with things that weren't pleasing to God. I understood that I made my own choices and had allowed situations to influence me, and whether I knew it was against God or not, I was creating my own record. And then even after God brought His word to me, I had still chosen to operate outside what He wanted, like I was negotiating with God.

"July 1997 was the last time I slept with a man outside of marriage. I went before the Lord and said, 'God, this is it. I've had enough of me. I've had enough of cutting corners, compromising, not waiting on you. I'm not including anyone else in this; this is me. I'm messy. I'm a mess. I want out. I need help. I really want to know you. I want to be born again in the spirit. I want to walk in your word, I want to walk in your power. I want to live a transparent life.' Every time I observe things about myself that are contrary to the word, I appeal to the Lord to help me. I try not to justify it, but just come to terms with what is."

In 1999, fifteen years after her old life began its downward spiral, Marsha Allen found a new one as an ordained and licensed minister. That year, she was named minister and administrator of the Global Church, a social service ministry based in Perris, California. Most of her work is with the Church's Peace Center for Family Advancement, aimed at supporting and preserving families at risk. The new position has given her a different network of movers and shakers, even taken her to the White House.

These days, she still conducts two-pronged seminars. But her "One Life to Live" module has been replaced by one titled "If God Said It, That Settles It." And the "Entrepreneurial Approach to Living" curriculum has given way to one called, simply, "True Repentance of Sin."

As before, Marsha is driven to do even more. Soon, she says, she will launch a project that will take her soul-saving mission worldwide. Though she's not sure when she will begin the work, Marsha knows whence its direction comes. She is certain that it was God's plan all along to press her into service and that caused opposing forces to step up the pressure on her to adhere to the lies, deceptions, and games it takes to score many worldly rewards. Marsha says she has never been as fulfilled and as at peace with herself as she is now.

Invariably, stories like these prompt the questions: Did God orchestrate the breakdown, the crisis, the dilemma? Are these modern versions of Paul (né Saul) being blinded on the road to Damascus? Was it His way of destroying the old self in order to let a new spirit emerge, a spirit tapped for a higher purpose?

That's the great riddle. And it's a classic one. Unfortunately, you'll find no answers here. I have no idea where God draws the line between our will and His. On this, not even people who have gone through hell and back have consensus. For example, Marsha believes God willed her collapse. "God was not going to allow me to go on in life and do my own things," Marsha told me. "He showed me that He would do whatever He had to do to bring me to a place of submission."

"He can choose you and give you the spirit of repentance so that you can begin to look at your life compared to His word and come to a place where you can have a broken and contrite heart," Marsha Allen says. "What can God do? He could keep me while the devil was at my heels and I didn't know it. What can God do? He allowed me to go through every kind of hardship related to sin and by the time I knew the truth about sin, I wasn't debating with Him. You know how people debate with the Lord—*Do I have to give up my cigarettes, do I have to give up fornication?* I was just saying, 'Help me give up.' What God can do if we repent is awesome."

7

The Last Campaign

S elf-assured though we may be, the fact is we cannot verify the legitimacy of purported spiritual conversion. There is no surefire monitoring system; it won't show up in a urine test. It's the confessor's word against our own judgment. But then, it's not our job to know; that's God's alone, though I imagine He tolerates our tendency to attempt measurement of another's faith by not only their profession of it but by their postconversion conduct. Yet I'm queasy about those judgments, too.

All I can say with certainty is that God can lift a person from the pits of any hell—the self-made hell and the unwitting hell, the physical hell, the emotional hell, the financial hell, the social hell. It's not a matter of believing what that person is capable of; it's knowing what God can do.

On January 29, 1982, the Reagan White House issued this notice:

The President today announced his appointment of Lee Atwater of Columbia, South Carolina, to be Deputy Assistant to the President for Political Affairs. . . . In his new position, Atwater will be the White House point man for the 1982 congressional elections.

Now, as everyone knows, when you move into the West Wing of the building that headquarters the world's greatest singular power, you are being acknowledged as an exceptional talent—a specialist—whom the president believes will advance, if not secure, his agenda.

Atwater's specialty was character assassination. He was, in effect, a political hit man for the Republican Party, and though barely in his thirties, he was already well known and widely feared in Washington. As a campaign strategist, he had several times demonstrated a knack for finding an opponent's weak spot and repeatedly striking him there until he fell. Atwater was known as a merciless antagonist, a scurrilous genius, a dangerous blend of southern charm and vicious spirit. There was nothing modest about Atwater. To the contrary, he relished his reputation as a maestro of down and dirty politics, bragged about it, hyped it. And why not? The gunslinger strategy had worked time and time again, depositing his candidates in office. More than that, it had taken him to the uppermost realm of American politics.

Fellow South Carolinian Tom Turnipseed, a Democratic state senator and lawyer, found himself in Atwater's crosshairs during a campaign for Congress in 1980.

"Atwater was a consultant for my opponent, the Republican incumbent," Turnipseed wrote in the *Washington Post* in 1991. "Atwater's antics included phony polls by 'independent pollsters' to 'inform' white suburbanites that I was a member of the NAACP . . . and last-minute letters from Sen. Strom Thurmond (R-S.C.) warning voters that I would disarm America and turn it over to the liberals and Communists."

According to Turnipseed, not even victory satisfied Atwater's mean streak. During the campaign, Atwater had made hay of Turnipseed's treatment—thirty-five years earlier—for adolescent depression, something the candidate had publicly acknowledged years before. As Turnipseed wrote, "Atwater had cultivated his macho image with the national media by telling about how he had planted a story with reporters covering the 1980 congressional race that I had been 'hooked up to jumper cables' when I was 'mentally ill' as a student. . . . Lee seemed to delight in making fun of a suicidal 16-year-old who was treated for depression with electroshock treatments."

In 1988, Atwater cemented his notorious reputation and carved his name into the annals of modern political history. Vice President George Bush was running for president that year, and as chairman of the Republican National Committee, Atwater was the campaign's mastermind. The chairman's coup de grâce was his suggestion that the Democratic nominee, Massachusetts governor Michael Dukakis, was responsible for the rape of a white woman by a black man who had recently been released from prison. In producing the infamous Willie Horton ads for television, Atwater employed menacing, shadowy visual effects and a haunting narrative. He cast Dukakis as reckless and spineless on crime and exploited racist fears. Atwater was proud of it.

But something happened in the middle of the 1990 midterm elections that would cause Lee Atwater to rethink his attitudes and approaches to life and work. On a trip to Puerto Rico, his runner's legs gave out. Shortly after that, he collapsed onstage during a fund-raising speech. Soon, a new, formidable and unexpected opponent announced itself—cerebrum astrocytoma, a brain tumor the size of an egg and already at grade three on a five-point pathology scale. At the time of discovery, Atwater was thirty-nine years old. Doctors said he might last a year.

Atwater first sought refuge in denial. But as his prognosis worsened, he turned to every port in the storm. According to biographer John Brady, "He tried massage therapists, dream therapists, guided-imagery tapes of waterfalls, audiotapes of organ music and waves crashing on the shore and acupuncture. He went to a psychiatrist. When a healer told Lee to get rid of his black T-shirts and start wearing red underwear, he did. Tibetan monks visited, studied Lee's urine, recommended creams and vitamin therapy."

As a last resort, Atwater turned to a spiritual counselor. Under her guidance, he professed that he had found God, announcing that "He's made a difference and I'm glad I've found Him while there's still time." Atwater renounced his old ways and began writing "forgiveness letters" and placing "forgiveness calls" to people he now believed he had wronged.

Tom Turnipseed received his letter from Atwater in June of 1990. In it, Atwater apologized for the "jumper cable episode" particularly, calling it "one of the low points" of his career.

"He said in his letter to me that 'my illness has taught me

something about the nature of humanity, love, brotherhood and relationships that I never understood and probably never would have. So, from that standpoint, there is some truth and good in everything,'" Turnipseed recalled in his *Washington Post* piece.

Early on the morning of March 29, 1991, Lee Atwater succumbed.

8

—

$\mathcal{D}$*eliverance*

I understand that some folks may not trust deathbed or jail-house conversions. They would view the claim of salvation under those conditions as, more probably, a convenience, a ruse, a gimmick with which to wrangle oneself out of a bind, whether that bind is what other people are going to do to you or what they're going to say about you.

Few examples of such cynicism are more naked than in the case of Karla Faye Tucker, convicted in the 1983 murders of Jerry Lynn Dean and Deborah Thornton in a Houston, Texas, apartment. The murders were astoundingly gruesome. Tucker's partner, Daniel Garrett, used a hammer while Tucker wielded a pickax that she left lodged in Thornton's bloodied and badgered torso.

By the time of her execution date more than fourteen years later, Tucker was known as an exemplary inmate. Moreover, she had established herself as a "born again" Christian devoted to leading other prisoners to Christ. Convinced that the woman's conversion was genuine, religious leaders of all faiths and from all over the world pleaded for commutation of her death sentence. Tucker seemed resigned to the possibility that her death at the hands of the State of Texas was imminent. Still, she made her own case for mercy. In a letter to then-governor George W. Bush, Tucker reasserted her guilt in the slayings as well as her commitment "to do right . . . not because I am in prison, but because my God demands this of me."

On a February evening in 1998, Tucker was strapped to a gurney in the execution chamber at Huntsville, Texas. She apologized to her victims' families, told her husband she loved him, and declared, "I'm going to be face-to-face with Jesus now." It took about eight minutes for the lethal cocktail of sodium thiopental, pancuronium bromide, and potassium chloride to end her life.

Later, someone wrote a Texas newspaper editor to say that he was among those who rejoiced over Tucker's execution and were not persuaded by her purported spiritual conversion. "All of these pleas for clemency were based on the notion that she had become a Born Again Christian," the man wrote. "The only thing to do on death row is find religion. After all, she was facing death and obviously had fear over what would happen afterward."

Suspicion is an understandable response to sudden conversions of any kind. But tell me: Is there a more likely place and time to find God, to call on Him, to believe in Him, to commit to Him, than when you are at rock bottom and everything is on the line—livelihood, life itself, the afterlife? Could there be a more perfect setup for conversion than being afraid, alone, in danger, wracked by guilt and shame, and out of options?

Of course, this kind of mercy is beyond our comprehension. By our standards, it may even seem preposterous, as in the case of the letter-writer in the Tucker case. He actually ended the letter saying that if Karla Faye Tucker could get into heaven, he didn't know if he wanted to go.

It's one thing to question how God forgives a person for such a vicious sin. It's quite another to question *that* He forgives. The writer could probably use a little of that unimaginable mercy for himself.

9

—

The Long Way Home

By the time Mary Edmonds gave birth to her third child in the summer of 1941, there were already two children in the small, struggling household in Edgecombe County, North Carolina. Mary's former husband, a man given to alcoholic rages and abuse, fathered her first son and daughter. The newest addition, a boy she named Wilbert, had a different father.

William Gaynor was an ex-navy man who had been trained as a baker during his military service. When he was discharged, he found a way to make a living off his kitchen skills, and that brought him a certain stature back home. In the rural South of the early twentieth century, most black men were farm laborers. Being a baker made Gaynor something of a big shot.

Like her father, Mary was endowed with natural musical talent. She was a good singer and became proficient at playing piano without the benefit of formal lessons. Artistically inclined, Mary felt boxed in by the small-town ways of Edgecombe County, and if her own ambitions and talents were not a vehicle to a better, more exciting life, then "marrying up" might be. For a while, William Gaynor looked like the ticket.

But the romance failed to blossom into a committed relationship. Gaynor impregnated Mary, but they never married. Thus, Wilbert was born to an unwed mother. She gave him her maiden name as a surname—Burgess. One year later, Mary had another baby, a girl, by a man she had gotten involved with while living in Washington, D.C., where her mother had relocated after she and Mary's father ended their marriage.

When the children were eight, seven, four, and three, Mary suffered a nervous breakdown back in North Carolina and was committed to what was then heartlessly known as "the state insane asylum." Her mother—the feisty, hardworking, go-get-'em Addie Burgess—came to fetch the children to live with her in the nation's capital, a crudely segregated city, but one where black workers could at least find jobs, however menial.

Wilbert recalls:

I remember she brought us back on the train. She had several pots of food because, you know we weren't given access to the dining car. I remember eating black-eyed peas and chicken and cabbage and stuff like that on the train. And I remember feeling kind of protected. I don't remember feeling like anything really, really, really bad had happened because everybody protected us.

When Grandma showed up, believe me, she pulled everybody together. She was the classic matriarch of the family— very strong matriarch whose power was never questioned.

The children settled in with Addie in a government-run housing project in Washington's predominantly black southwest
quadrant, an enclave of poor people scrambling to keep hearth
and home together under Jim Crow. Wilbert remembers it as
"classic ghetto," just around the corner or across the street from
a nest of ragged and dangerous slums.

Addie got welfare assistance to help provide for her grandchildren and her own daughter who lived in the home, the
youngest of her nine surviving children. Addie worked, too. She
was a charwoman at the old Department of Health, Education,
and Welfare (renamed Health and Human Services after Education became a separate department of the executive branch).
And on Thursdays, she worked for a wealthy white family on
Butternut Street in upper-crust northwest Washington.

Says Wilbert:

*Grandma would bring food home from the Butternut
Street house. I mean, she would have no less than three
shopping bags with all kinds of goodies in it. When I would
see her, it was like she had this aura around her.*

*She would also entertain us with all these stories about
those strange people she worked for—the nonsense that
they would be fussing about and haggling over when it just
seemed like they had nothing else to do. They would quib-
ble over the tiniest things and she would sometimes be
called upon to settle silly little quarrels. Grandma always
described them as just silly. She said they were so rich and
they had so much going on, that they lost all their common*

sense. I'm quite sure my grandmother had no appreciation of what was happening in the stock market or the fashion world or the things that might have concerned them. So the stuff she was hearing that seemed so weighty to them always seemed so trivial to her.

The other thing she talked about was how wasteful they were. They would have her prepare all this food when there was no way in the world they could eat it all. Then they would cut a few slices off the ham or the roast and let Grandma take the rest home. Well, I'm sure the woman did that on purpose sometimes. They would want lavish meals, but there wasn't even an issue about whether they were going to eat it all. They would use food and clothing and such as gifts to the help. But when it came to food, it was, "I work for these people who are really sinfully wasteful, but we're not like that. We appreciate what the Lord has given us." She was teaching us to be thrifty, not to be wasteful, to be grateful to God. To this very day, I detest waste. I know that is from the way I grew up.

Wilbert was a preteen the first time he laid eyes on his father, William Gaynor, and even then it was a business matter that brought them together.

Not long before they met, the welfare department had begun cracking down on noncustodial fathers who had not been supporting their children. The agency ordered a roundup of abdicators, pressuring the children's mothers or guardians to produce the men for an accounting or else face a loss of benefits.

To their chagrin and his, Wilbert's older half brother and

half sister were sent back to North Carolina "to live with their crazy, alcoholic father." The father of his younger half sister was nearby and Addie worked out a payment arrangement with him.

That left Wilbert, who came home from school one day to find a strange man in his grandmother's house.

Says Wilbert:

My grandmother called me into the room and said, "This is your father. Turn around and let him see you." So I did the 360, let him look me over like a prized calf. I didn't like that one bit. After I turned around for him, I left the room. I heard him tell Grandma, "Well, he can come down to North Carolina but he can't stay in the house with us because my wife, she has these children and they're all light-skinned and she's light-skinned, so he wouldn't fit in. He can live in the house right across the path; he can stay there."

My grandmother wanted to know what I thought about that after he left. I basically told her he could stick it. By that time, I was eleven years old, I was doing fine with Grandma and this dude comes in with some shaky deal like that. So Grandma made some kind of arrangement with him to get him off the hook, some kind of payment agreement which allowed her to keep me with her. She more or less covered for him, I think.

Not only was he "doing fine," Wilbert was thriving in school. From the start, he excelled in his studies and so outpaced his classmates that, when he completed first grade, Wilbert was assigned directly to grade three. School officials wanted to "skip" the boy again later, but he would have had to move to a school out of walking range from home. Besides, he says, his young aunt was already resentful of her older sister's children, whom she considered interlopers.

Says Wilbert:

She was very resentful of four children being brought in all of a sudden when she pretty much had Grandma all to herself. In fact, Grandma was always afraid to give us too much attention because we had this little jealous aunt there. This was her last child and she doted on her. The aunt was a brat, actually. She tortured us when Grandma was away. She would force us to play these games where she was the "king." She would make my older sister, who was a year younger than her, the "queen" and let her serve as head honcho or executioner to punish anyone violating the king's laws.

My brother would really get it. They would tie him up with clothesline and put him in the closet and lock him in. And then they would take pins and stick him all over his body. This was practically a daily thing. I remember being in that closet a couple of times, too. It might not sound like much then, but for a vulnerable child, it was pretty traumatic. Even today, when my brother talks about that, his eyes glaze over.

But kids have an amazing survival mechanism, you know? Because, guess what? My brother and I worked up a thing for when we got closet time. We would go through all the pockets of the clothes in the closet and we would

find pennies and nickels. That little game made it bear-
able . . . until the "executioner" came to torture us again.

Among his peers, Wilbert was a popular, semi-celebrity—"a little star" locally recognized for his beautiful soprano voice. His
reputation as a good singer kept some of the neighborhood
roughnecks at bay since they respected him as "the little singing
guy."

He liked his modest fame and reveled in the excitement of
frequent performances with the school chorus. One particular
teacher thought Wilbert was going places. She showed up one
evening to discuss some proposition with Addie—Wilbert
never knew exactly what, only that it was a great opportunity
for him—but nothing ever came of it. "My family either didn't
know what to do or some money or resources were required,
they just didn't have it," he says. Not that his household ever
took his singing talent seriously.

Says Wilbert:

In the environment I grew up in, my gifts and talents were
not appreciated. They were treated as kind of a joke. So
both the gifts and the abusive things were treated as if they
weren't happening.

Even when I was a kid, I was very aware and very alert,
wondering why the authority figures weren't doing their
job. Why we weren't really being protected despite this
whole facade of being protected. Looking at it with a
child's mind, I developed a distrust of people in authority, I
suppose because the main people in authority in my life

were looking the other way for whatever reason. But I al-
ways remained cheerful; it's just a God-given thing I guess.
I always could see humor. Most people would never know
how hurt and afraid and distrustful I was because I was
smiling on the outside, but on the inside I was, like, "When
is help going to show up?"

In my own way, I rebelled. In fact I spent most of my life
as a rebel. A lot of it was passive aggression because you can
be sure that the only aggression that would be safe with
Grandma was passive. My brother used to run away and
stay out of the house, but I went inward. I would stay out of
the way. There was no running away or going anywhere for
me because the world was too big and scary.

Perhaps it was the series of dejections, disappointments, disin-
terest, and neglect of his talents and ambitions that led to
Wilbert's habit of rejecting kindnesses, a classic sign of crippled
self-esteem.

It became his custom, when being recognized at church, at
school, or in the community for musical or scholastic achievement, to simply not show up to receive the plaque, the ribbon,
the award, the praise. He's analytical about it now. "Honestly,
after having all of my essential accomplishments ignored for all
those years by people I cared most about, I started kind of working in reverse," he explained. "Plus, there was so much envy. In
order to live with the people I was surrounded by, I had to kind
of play it down, to underachieve. I couldn't stand to be blessed
when I couldn't take everybody with me." Indeed, any gratification Wilbert may have had was invariably drowned by guilt.

As a grown man, he once picked an argument with his girl-friend who wanted to purchase a painting for him as a birthday present. "I chewed her out because my mother was still in a rest home and here I am in a sports car, running around, and now she wants to buy this fancy artwork. I asked her, 'Couldn't you think of something a little less ostentatious?' It was ridiculous, but I was afraid to live too good."

Nonetheless, opportunity continued to knock occasionally on Wilbert's door. Shortly after the U.S. Supreme Court abolished segregation in public schools with its 1954 ruling in the landmark *Brown v. Board of Education* case, Wilbert enrolled in Washington's highly regarded Dunbar High School, then a bastion of white privilege. The curriculum was new and heady stuff for Wilbert—four years of Latin, four years of French, economics, and the humanities. With those courses on his record and good grades to boot, Wilbert was primed for college. He chose Howard, the university that had educated a stream of black achievers, including, at its law school, the lead attorney in the *Brown* case, future Supreme Court Justice Thurgood Marshall. But while Wilbert's future looked promising, clouds were slowly gathering.

Says Wilbert:

When I got to Howard, I fell in love right away with a girl from Chicago. We met on campus. She was an artist. Of course I was an artist, too, but I didn't really understand that I was. We just kind of glommed on to each other. We were desperately in love, but also such victims of where we came from and who our parents were. Her parents were both alcoholics. They had broken up. Her father was hanging out on the streets, drinking wine. Her mom was back in Chicago doing her thing and had sent her two daughters to live with their grandmother. That was certainly familiar.

We were so needy, both of us. But if you will just wipe away all of that and just be a total romantic and just look at two young people who very passionately tried to love each other, that's the story I like. We wanted to be married to each other. But there were a lot of things going on in the background.

I had picked up some drinking buddies who were also a bunch of high-achieving guys who all went on to get advanced degrees. Except me. Because this woman and I were so into each other, we forgot about academic pursuits. So I flunked out and dropped out in 1962 and went to work at the post office. It was just a matter of time before the relationship broke down. Now, I'm out of a relationship, I'm kind of depressed, but suddenly I'm making all of this money, relatively speaking. So I decide to be Mr. Magnanimous. I'm still hanging out on campus and I have this one friend who's a struggling artist. I decided that since I hadn't made it in school, I was going to help this guy. So just this one time, he couldn't get his registration money together— it was like a couple of hundred dollars—and I helped him so he could stay in school. He went on to graduate pretty much on time.

I was kind of rescued at that point by Uncle Sam. In 1964, Uncle Sam said "Stop everything; if you want to help somebody succeed, help me for two years." That was kind of a blessing in disguise. It got me off my treadmill for a couple of years. In fact, the woman I was in love with got married that Saturday and I had to report that Monday to boot camp in February of '64.

But when I came back out of the service, this woman and I were right back at it again. She was married and there we were, tipping around. For the next fifteen years, we were in and out of each other's lives. During that time, she was in two different marriages and she was living with some man, some gangster. I was still hung up on her.

I made a couple more attempts to finish school, but I was getting into the drinking thing more, though in my mind I was just partying. But the fact of the matter was, I never again tried to really get in a serious relationship. I spent at least the next ten or fifteen years just kind of screwing around. Because, first of all, "she" was always out there somewhere and I don't think we would have allowed each other to have a good relationship with anyone else because there was always the issue called "us."

Some people in my family think that was a major turning point in my life. But what I was to learn later on was that all of this stuff was like sleepwalking. Sometimes I think from the time I witnessed my mother in the breakdown situation, I think that I was walking through life almost in a survival mode; on automatic pilot. I could not say that I had a conscious grip on my life and what direction I was trying to take. I was basically going through the motions.

• • •

Wilbert had first wanted to be a psychiatrist—"to help my mother and people like her," he said—but then decided social work was his calling. Music was still in his soul, but Wilbert didn't see much chance of earning a living with his voice.

In 1968, he took a job as a counselor at a halfway house for drug abusers. He poured himself into the work and soon came to understand the people who had a way of life that he had been able to avoid even though it had festered in every alley and around every corner of his childhood.

Says Wilbert:

I saw what Grandma never allowed us to see. She told us, "Those boys on the corner? Those are bad boys and you stay away from them." So I never knew what their day-to-day lives were like until I became a counselor at age twenty-four or twenty-five and got to know them and started reading their files. These kids are playing cowboys and Indians and cops and robbers with the cops out here. And yet these people are always blamed.

My education had trained me to be a professional who would have to deal with people like this, but always from the perspective that they had created their own circumstances and were responsible for their conditions.

Well, I threw all of that out the window. By this time, I was becoming a social activist. In working with the boys, I'm not really trained for that. I'm bringing my personality there, I'm bringing my empathy and whatever else I've got. I think I'm a reasonably effective counselor; but not really, because I really don't know who I am.

But Wilbert's private habits—the drinking, the promiscuous sex, the marijuana smoking—were taking their toll, grinding down his spirit, his health, and his career. By 1973, he hit the wall. He walked around in an alcohol- and drug-induced fog most of the time, he became lax at work, and he was convinced that a drug dealer was out to get him. To add to his troubles, Wilbert—thirty-two years old by this time—had gotten into a messy relationship with a seventeen-year-old girl with two small children.

Says Wilbert:

At this point I'm working as a counselor, very involved in the community. In the course of that work, I find out about this girl living in a roach-infested place. She's got two babies from two different men and nobody's trying to step up to the plate. And she is showing signs of being a little suicidal or she's about ready to throw one of the babies out of the window or something. When I go over to visit her, the door is unlocked. Well, I can't take this; I've got to make sure she and the children are safe. So I rented a U-Haul and moved mama, babies, roaches, rats, everything. I moved all of them over here to my house. My neighbors started referring to her as my "niece," so I never bothered to correct them. I guess they interpreted it that way because they figured, "I know Mr. Burgess ain't lost his mind."

Now, I really believed that I was just doing her a favor, that she needed maybe a couple of months to get herself together. I'm still willing to defend myself that when I brought her home, it wasn't just as a new sex toy. But that's pretty much what it became. We had a daily ritual, however. I would come in from work, she was supposed to be looking for work, and I would find her sitting on the sofa next to the front door with the classified section opened wide.

Four months went by and she's still there. During that time, I think we had at least one pregnancy scare. But she's not going anywhere. I can't get her to move. Nothing worked. What I had to eventually do was put the house up for rent and move around the corner. But, you know what? She befriended the people I rented the house to; she was over there hanging out with them. To make a long story short, I don't think I had been at my new apartment but a couple of months when she moved in over there, too. I moved her in.

It got to the point where she would disappear for a few days right after the first of the month when her welfare check came in. Then she would come back home and say she had been kidnapped either by one of her babies' fathers or one of their friends. She did this at least twice. Uh huh, right. So I said, "From now on, to keep you from getting 'kidnapped,' you give me the check at the first of the month and I'm going to save your money and get you your own place." That's what I did.

It took two years for Wilbert to come to his senses and break off from the young woman for good. By then, his friends had lost respect for him, his college education had been scuttled, and even though he had taken a solid, mid-grade job in the federal government, "I'm in the process of blowing it because my out-side behavior is making it harder and harder to stay on the ca-reer ladder."

Says Wilbert:

If you have a certain amount of intellectual capacity, you can create a kind of identity for yourself, but your behavior will tell where you are at an emotional level. There was a lot about that relationship that said a lot about who I was and where I came from. It showed me I wasn't equipped to get into a conventional relationship with myself or anyone else. By the time I came out of that situation, I had lost sight of the world.

The next few years were, to put it mildly, unstable. Wilbert managed to keep a job and a roof over his head, but he was un-enthusiastic about work and, from appearances at least, devoid of real ambition. Most of his energies went into feeding his worsening alcohol and marijuana habits and his reputation as a ladies' man. Walking on the wild side, he had more than a few brushes with danger.

Says Wilbert:

At one point, I'm sneaking around with this woman mar-ried to a drug dealer who is known to carry at least a .38 with him wherever he goes. Meanwhile, I am appalled at even taking a Swiss knife with me, and besides, it's not even in my nature to do violent things. And there we are, riding along the parkway, holding hands, in love.

*Now, I'm coming back with this woman from some-
where and we go to the house of a cousin who is keeping
this woman's children. She tells us the old man—the drug
dealer—just left with a couple of his buddies, beating
down her door, talking about, "Give me back my kids."
They had just left as we were coming in. They took the
stairs; we took the elevator. And when I realized how close
a call that was, I figured God was definitely protecting me
that day.*

By 1980, his life was in such a downward spiral that rock bottom was only a hairsbreadth away. Desperate and afraid,
Wilbert turned to the twelve steps of Alcoholics and Narcotics
Anonymous for rescue. The programs shook him back to his
senses. And helped put him back in touch with the God his
grandmother Addie had praised all her life.

Says Wilbert:

*The way they do the twelve-step thing, from day one,
they're holding you accountable. Some people never learn
to take responsibility for themselves. And I had a whole
long list of people who harmed me in some way. What I
learned in recovery is that you run the information
through, be very clear about what the issues were and who
did what, but you still have the responsibility of picking up
the pieces and going forward. As far as the people who
harmed you are concerned, drop the charges. If you use
them as an excuse for why you're still drinking and doping
and knocking your old lady upside the head, you're still a*

victim. Plus, even if you haven't decided you're responsible,
society has been holding you accountable.

You start recognizing how totally self-centered and self-
pitying you've become in your life and that you've totally
made a lifestyle out of this business of being a victim. And
you don't know, it doesn't really bother you that you're
throwing away all of this power because you've only had a
little taste of it and never experienced it with any consis-
tency. But, little by little, they teach you to taste this thing.

The day that you really get it and you understand that
they're trying to get you to reconnect with your God
source, you can take off and take bigger steps and finally let
go of living according to your baggage and start living in
the present.

The support and lessons he took from the Alcoholics and Narcotics Anonymous programs inspired Wilbert to return to the
church. He was determined to reconnect with God and soon
became a fixture in a large Washington, D.C., congregation.

It was a double blessing for Wilbert. Not only did church
life give him a sense of security, purpose, and righteousness, it
also gave him an opportunity to exercise one of his greatest pas-
sions—singing. He took delight in the music ministry's new
Men's Chorus, though, for the first couple of years, the group
had a repertoire of only about three songs.

The Union Temple's Men's Chorus has since become large,
renown, and semiprofessional. Wilbert Burgess is one of several

regular soloists who move audiences with their soulful renditions of Negro spirituals, popular anthems, and both old-time and progressive gospel. The Chorus has performed all over America and maintains a full schedule of engagements at myriad political, civic, and religious events in and around the nation's capital.

It was during an appearance at a church in Maryland that Wilbert says God changed his heart for good. Until that day in the early 1990s, he had, like many struggling believers, been leading something of a double life, reaching for God with one hand, holding on to worldly temptations and delights with the other. Says Wilbert:

We were in concert at some church out in the country and, you know us, big old Union Temple, we're like, "Oh, how quaint; thank goodness, they're going to get some good entertainment tonight because we're cool."

And one of these boys—we called him "Bam Bam"—he couldn't read or write but he had a body that was right out of the box and he was getting a lot of play from the women. He had a rich, beautiful baritone voice. This guy had groupies. We all had our groupies but he had those loud, get up, forget-where-they-are groupies. He opens up and they're out of control, screaming, "Sing, Bam Bam; sing!"

We were into the program; Bam Bam had sung once or twice, the women are really getting wild and I was really getting scared. We had been having a good career, working all over; we were well known and popular. But this particular night, we were really taking it over the top to the point where I was really scared. And I started thinking, "You by yourself. And He will reward you for doing that because you'll find out that He is there and He is real and all that power that you gave away all your life, that's over with. He says, "You come to me about power issues. You'll find out where the power station is. They can't get between me and you. All you have to do is keep your eyes on me and I will give you peace." That's the lesson I learned that night. But I learned it by doing it. Because I couldn't go any further the way I had been going.

It's amazing how that changed my life. And that was something that had nothing to do with nothing except for a need I had within myself to cry out to God. That tells me the particulars of your life make good filler. But God will step in at any point you call on Him and neutralize your problems and put you back on the path.

Once you have made that connection, it's clear. We've been hearing all our lives, put God first. We hear it on an intellectual level. But when you get it from your spirit reaching out to the Great Spirit, it's a whole lot of peace.

Materially, Wilbert is comfortable. Not rich, not wealthy, not set for life, just comfortable. He's still a working stiff, devoted to faith-based community service. But spiritually, he is a rich man.

Some of his old college pals have forged highly successful careers. They are doctors and lawyers and engineers and professors. Many of them are also involved in community service and church work. But Wilbert wonders what became of one particular old friend.

Says Wilbert:

know what? We are showing out so bad that God is going to take a position." And I started praying, "God, I don't want to be a part of this, and if you're really there, I need to hear from you tonight." Because instead of being a blessing or something that was taking us closer to God, I'm thinking, here we are in church, really begging for a shot of hell. And I don't want to do this. I don't want to be a part of this. Just before my time to go up front to lead a song, I started praying intensely. I just sort of lost track of where I was. I asked God to touch me. I said, "For once in my life, I don't care what anybody thinks, I just need to hear from you. If being all up in yourself and ego-tripping, if it leads to this kind of madness, I don't want any part of it." I told God, "If I never do it again, I'm going to sing this just for you."

I tell you, something washed over me. I can't even describe it. Everything was going on around me, but I was in my own little space. I just felt like I had been cleansed of something. And for the first time ever, I decided I'm not worrying about being cool or hitting that high note or any of that. For once, I didn't look around to see who was into me, who was on the right note. I just did what I do. I had been singing all my life; the singing part I knew. Letting go, I didn't know. That was the first time I had totally abandoned myself to God. From that time on, I've been my own man in my relationship with God. No man comes between me and my God. He came through for me that night. What I asked him for, he gave me.

When it comes to dealing with God, you can't bring your mama and your daddy and your brother, you've got to come

There was this one really brilliant cat, this really intellec-
tual guy I used to hang around in college. He was deep
into the existentialists—Nietzsche, Sartre—and he could
just whip you down in intellectual discourse with these
highbrow concepts. Come to think of it, this was when
everyone was talking about "finding yourself." Come to
think of it, this was the same time they were saying, "God
is dead." Coincidence? I don't think so.

Anyway, I would get into these discussions sometimes
with this existentialist brother and he would not want to
hear this talk about God. I was not really on the right
course yet, but I did have some grasp of God and religious
faith. After all, I was raised by Addie Burgess and she was a
God-fearing woman, no doubt. And she made sure we
knew about Him, too.

But this brother would just come apart in these discussions.
This brilliant, accomplished, deep-thinking guy couldn't deal
with that old, second-grade-education Addie Burgess Jesus.
He would just come apart. With all his education and exis-
tentialism, he couldn't handle her Jesus.

Wilbert says one of his greatest fears about giving up the high
life for the good life was that he would miss the fun and thrills
of life on the streets. But his spirituality has given him a new
support group—a steady stream of "cousins" in the faith, as he
calls them.

It puts you in touch with millions and millions of kindred
spirits. Before you take that step, you think this is going to be

a lonely thing. Yeah, if you're a coward. But you find out
there are many spirits out here making communion with God.
And loneliness is not an issue, even though you may be alone.

While Wilbert Burgess is committed to his new walk, he acknowledges that negotiating the straight and narrow can be
tricky. Temptations beckon at every resting place, lurk at every
turn, flashing their bright lights in hopes that he blinks or takes
his eyes off the road.

No matter how life can be so convoluted and so confusing,
if that's where you are, if you're stuck in the madness,
you're distracted. All of this stuff is available, it's right
there. But you're so distracted that you're missing it. I've
often heard sermons where the minister's talking about
how the devil tries to distract you to keep you from tuning
in to what God is trying to say to you. Ego pleasures. At-
tention. Fortune. Fame or whatever to simply distract.

So many of the classic stories, biblical plays, the core stuff
is about folly. They make a point that we are so susceptible
to being totally distracted by other ways of seeing life that
seems to make sense. And the Bible says there is a way that
seemeth right unto a man. But the end of the way is death.

I've held on to that. I said that's my story because I al-
ways felt that what I was doing is right. But then I could
see myself being pushed more and more toward destruc-
tion. Yes, you may be thoroughly convinced that what
you're doing is right. That's okay; that's part of being
human. But allow for the fact that you could be wrong.

I tell you, when you truly take that first step, not only does He put people in your life; He puts a group of them. Total strangers come up to me, as if they were given an assignment to meet some strange guy in the lobby and tell him something and maybe plant one little piece of wisdom. I've had people that I've seen for the first time in my life respond to me as if they were there to give me that message. And it was something about me that told them they should, in spite of the fact that they've never seen me before, share with me in a certain way. I think it has something to do with the fact that that night years ago I asked God to reveal some things to me. Even today, when I get distracted from that, I get nothing. When I get on the beam, I get all kinds of insights flooding in.

My biggest challenge today is to be ready for all the blessings that I'm looking at. Because it is a very real thing when you've lived all those years avoiding blessings. And as you move forward in your life, you find yourself in the company of people who are more productive and more comfortable with positive living and it's definitely less and less of a challenge. It's good to be able to tell a story where you were so lost and so confused and just hated anything about having faith and hearing "the Lord will provide" and now, through His grace, you can tell that story yourself. I tell you . . .

Wilbert goes silent. Then, "Lord have mercy." Then a long, deep sigh.

Buoyed by his own testimony, the singer melts into song. *"Wouldn't take nothing for my journey now,"* he croons. *"Wouldn't take nothing for my journey now, Mount Zion."*

10

—

Scrub Work

His friends called him "Powder" after the character in a 1995 movie by that name—an albino teen who had extrasensory powers and who held on to his virtue, strong conscience, and warm heart despite being, himself, mistreated by his peers. Powder was an outcast.

That was not Matthew, however. He got the nickname only because his fair skin and fair hair reminded one of his pals of the movie character. Matt didn't have special powers. Nor was his a warm heart. Far from it. Had it been, Matt would not have been much use to the skinheads.

By some estimates, there are somewhere between three thousand and ten thousand active skinheads in America. No one knows for sure how many there are because the organization operates in the shadows and the underground, a necessity if skinheads are to dodge the law and public reprisals for their predatory and sometimes deadly work.

The first skinheads were organized in Great Britain in the late 1960s. Their clean-shaven heads, steel-toed Doc Marten boots, suspenders, flight jackets, and distinctive tattoos identified them. The original skinheads celebrated working-class lifestyles and values. Many were school dropouts who felt alienated by the educated classes, especially as their blue collars became endangered at the advent of the electronic age. Eventually, skinhead groups began to oppose immigrants, especially nonwhite immigrants, who, they believed, gobbled up services and jobs to which they felt entitled by dint of nativity. With their resentment and anger premised on that sense of entitlement and tied to race, skinhead groups soon became identified with white supremacy.

By the time it had jumped the Atlantic and grabbed onto disaffected American youth, the skinhead movement had become known, first and foremost, for its racist component. Though there are skinheads who denounce racism and who are little more than a clique of boisterous, antiestablishment rebels, most skinhead organizations in the United States are preoccupied with white supremacy. They are violently opposed to interracial dating, interracial marriage, and even interracial friendship and association, claiming that each foretells a "mongrelization" of Caucasian peoples and, eventually, the "downfall" of the race.

The skinheads are, by any definition, a gang, operating outside the confines of proper society and often against the law. Like the notorious Crips, Bloods, Vice Lords, and Disciples who have stalked and ravaged poor neighborhoods across the country since the 1980s, skinheads have a hierarchy to their organization, a series of rituals and a code of conduct. Unlike other street gangs, skinheads are vehemently opposed to illegal drugs and have no commercial enterprises like dope peddling. They prefer alcohol—to use, not to sell—and they regularly get drunk together to underscore their solidarity. Like other gangs, skinheads are ruthlessly territorial. Only instead of a block or a neighborhood or a subdivision, the skinheads claim the echelons of privilege as their turf. Thus, they despise nonwhites, particularly blacks and Latinos, and homosexual whites because, according to skinhead philosophy, their sexual orientation robs the white race of potential to propagate.

Matt Bishop was ripe for recruitment. He was young, white, male, poor, disinterested in school, aimless, and fuming inside. His family was hardscrabble working class. His best friend had been killed in a car accident. His older brother was a gangbanger and drug user who stole from the family to finance his habit. Matt faulted his brother for his devilment, but more than that, he blamed the street life that had lured him into its snare. And more than that, he blamed the black youths who ran that life.

One night, at a friend's apartment, Matt met Chris, a young man in his twenties who was fluent in racism. Matt knew something of Chris from his Internet searches for information on white supremacist, white identity groups. He knew that Chris was a mid-level official in the skinhead movement, so to speak—a unit coordinator for the International Alliance. To Matt, Chris's message was music. He was mesmerized by the

older fellow's rants against alleged infringements by blacks, Latinos, non-Christians, and gays. He was excited by the man's exaltation of white rights, white power, and white privilege. He found the talk of a cause—preservation of the white race—seductive.

So at the tender age of thirteen, Matt Bishop joined the Norse Pagan unit of the International Alliance of Skinheads. For the first time in a long time, he felt he was where he belonged.

Encouraged by his newfound fraternity, Matt wasted no time proving his fitness for the group. Having been on the fringes of violent, supremacist groups, he was happy to actually hold membership among young men and women who shared his seemingly boundless anger and wrenching frustrations. He earned his stripes in the group when, at age sixteen, he got into a scrap with a black teen. In a move reminiscent of one of the darkest periods of American history—the lynching era that had scarred the first quarter of twentieth-century America—Matt threatened his adversary with a noose. An ensuing conviction for terroristic threats got Matt nine months in a juvenile detention center. But rather than repent, Matt left the facility with even more anger than before. He was also more convinced that the skinheads were for him. That sentiment was only affirmed when his fellow Norse Pagans treated him like a hero for the attack and for having survived incarceration. They cheered and toasted him. He got letters of admiration from fellow skinheads across the nation. Matt's stature rose immediately in the group; others looked up to him. He wallowed in the attention and accolades.

During his junior year in high school, Matt quit school. It had been ages since he was interested in his studies; he didn't care for most of his teachers; and he hated having to sit near black students or bump into them in the corridors between classes. Besides, there was work to be done for the movement—the labor of seething racism. There were black people to terrorize and gays to assault and other things that needed to be done to assert white authority. And there were, as always, the drunken gatherings that sometimes ended with one of the skinheads slapping or beating his wife or girlfriend, never mind the skinhead creed that, as the bearers of white children, white women are sacred.

Matt's family was aware of his new association. They knew what he was up to. His mother pleaded with him to leave the group, cautioning him that hatred was wrong and would eventually destroy him along with the lives upon which he preyed. The family also worried that Matt's baby brother, just a toddler, might follow in the footsteps of the big brother he adored.

Matt only dug in deeper. He took part in every bit of violence and lawlessness the group could contrive. He made no effort to hide his skinhead association, flouting the swastika that had been carved into his back by his late friend and the twin symbols on his arm: side-by-side marks resembling the lightning bolts that were the insignia of the Nazi "Schutzstaffel"—the elite military unit of Adolf Hitler's Third Reich. Commonly known as the "SS," the Schutzstaffel had, among other things, supervised the death camps where millions of Jews had perished. The letters S.W.P. were tattooed above the Nazi symbols. They stand for "southern white pride."

The more he unleashed his anger, the angrier Matt became. His fury fed upon itself, intensifying with each new act of violence and rebellion. Not even praise and respect from his peers could still the resentment and rage roiling inside him. He maintained his allegiance and full-fledged involvement in the group, but Matt was miserable.

To make matters worse, a voice was beginning to pipe up inside Matt's head. It challenged him, questioned him, and even scolded him. For the first time since he joined the skinheads, Matt was disturbed by fits of conscience. He began to see the danger and cruelty of his actions. Guilt and remorse haunted him. He started to lose patience with his friends' single-mindedness, their drunkenness, and their mistreatment of the women in their lives. Preying upon hapless gay men and black people no longer brought the satisfactions it once did. And he was tired of breaking his mother's heart.

Nonetheless, Matt soldiered on, hoping to recoup the high he used to feel when his buddies slapped him on the back or raised a glass to him in praise of some new treachery in the name of "the cause." But nothing would silence that little voice, growing louder and more frequent now, and nothing would calm the turbulence Matt felt in his gut.

Then one day Matt's mother was robbed and roughed up. He was livid. But before he could launch a plan of revenge, he learned that a black man had witnessed the attack and had come to his mother's rescue. Later, that man would work tirelessly to see that the assailant was caught and punished.

The voice in Matt's head was insistent now. Abandoning questions, it now made declarative statements: *Racism is wrong.*

Hatred is wrong. The skinheads are leading you to destruction. You are squandering your life. You need to get right with your family. You need to get right with God. The voice angered Matt. But he couldn't make it stop.

Eventually, Matt's resistance wore down. He began, slowly, to distance himself from the skinheads, not showing up for certain rituals or drinking binges; excusing himself from some of the group's assault and vandalism sprees. For some reason, he could not tear himself away from the skinheads entirely, but embarked upon a weaning process and step-by-step parted company with the crew and its vile philosophy.

"Things just started happening," Matt says, explaining his transformation. "Everybody has their own personal conscience, but God, I believe, was behind it one hundred percent. At the level I was involved in, there was no way that if something wasn't there powerful enough to pull me out, I wouldn't have gotten out of it. I know it was Him who made me see the light. I didn't want to see it at first, but He overpowered me."

As Matt began to withdraw from the skinheads, he made amends with his estranged family. They were relieved by his decision to pull out of the skinheads and encouraged Matt to rebuild his life. But there were still problems ahead. He had no education. He had no job. As far as he could see, he had no future. It was tempting to turn back to the skinheads—at least with them he had people who looked up to him and a way to while away the endless hours. But that voice propelled him forward, uncertain though he was of where he was headed. For a time, he held a low-paying job and moved in with his girlfriend, even talked about getting married. But seven dollars an hour was meager earnings and the relationship was strained by destitution until it broke. Matt was determined to get his life together. But how and where?

One day in the spring of 2003, shortly before he severed all ties with the skinheads, nineteen-year-old Matt set out on foot to his stepmother's workplace to fetch a house key. It was a long walk and, soon exhausted, he stopped an off-duty police officer and asked for a ride the rest of the way. The cop refused.

A passerby witnessed the exchange and, intrigued, approached Matt and offered him a ride to his stepmother's office. The man was curious about Matt's tattoos. Were they skinhead insignia? he asked as they drove through downtown. Yes, Matt replied, explaining what the movement was about and why he had become a part of it.

As Matt would soon learn, this was no ordinary stranger. Steve Nawojczyk was something of a legend. For nearly a decade, he had devoted his energies to leading wayward youth out of the thicket of gangs, drugs, violence, and aimlessness. Time after time, Steve had wandered into dens of dangerous youth that others dared not approach. Time after time, he had emerged into the clearing with some of those gangbangers in tow, full of trepidation but willing to try life in the mainstream. Steve helped them locate housing and jobs. He got them back in school. He helped them access recreational outlets and health care. Over all, he helped them reconcile with the society they had turned against and which, to no minor degree, had turned against them.

Steve knew how to read between the lines of hard talk that

typically spilled from gang members' mouths. He could discern yearning and fear and regret. He could sense desperation and need. He could tell when a kid wanted out and when he or she was ready to start over. He could tell Matt was ready. What he had to do first, Steve knew, was to hear Matt out.

"He got very talkative and it went from there," Steve recalled. "The kid knew huge amounts of skinhead philosophy. Now he was seeing through it, or at least beginning to." The two men quickly forged a friendship. Steve was determined to help Matt cut the last strings with the skinheads. He saw in Matt an uneducated but bright young man who deserved a better lot than he had gotten and who, he believed, was primed for change.

On their first outing together, Steve took Matt to the kind of gathering that represented all that Matt was not. He took him to the annual Boys State convention, where an elite corps of high school–aged males gathers for mock government exercises. Though they were his contemporaries, the delegates at Boys State could not have been more different from Matt. They were all exceptional students and school leaders, the cream of the crop, and all were viewed as future captains of government and big business. Bill Clinton had been a national Boys State delegate. Indeed, it was as a Boys Stater that young Clinton shook hands with President John F. Kennedy in the Rose Garden, a brief encounter that was captured in a now-famous photograph.

It goes without saying that, at the convention, Matt was out of his element. But he went to hear Steve's motivational speech to the convention. At one point, Steve made a motion to Matt that, unbeknownst to the audience, was a prearranged signal for Matt to come up and say a few words about self-determination in the face of temptations and dark urges. But Matt demurred. He later told Steve he was too nervous to speak before the crowd of one thousand strangers. But he had taken Steve's message to heart. In fact, he said, several parts of the lecture had given him goose bumps.

Next, Steve helped Matt retrieve his high school transcript so he could enroll in a G.E.D. class and earn a high school equivalency diploma. And he "hand delivered" him to the Job Corps, a job training and placement program for disadvantaged youth that has been around since Lyndon Johnson's Great Society.

Even with Steve's determined assistance, Matt's trip back to a positively charged, productive life has been laden with bumps and obstacles. But the little voice that used to annoy him has become his best friend. It keeps him going forward, looking up, believing that he can make it and that he will.

"Hate feels like somebody's inside of you eating you up," Matt says, reflectively. "It feels like there's an eternal fire in you. Out of all the things I had done—all the drinking and beating the hell out of people—it never released any of the hate; it just made it worse."

The fire is out now. Matt no longer hates. In fact, he repudiates it. He denounces the skinhead way of life and all the pain it represents. He is grateful for the second chance. Grateful, especially, that the God force was stronger than the dark and evil one that, for a time, owned his soul.

Poetry has become his new release. Dark poetry at first. Words and thoughts that have spilled out of his heart and, in the process, cleansed it. The work is "slowly getting lighter," he says.

"My really close friend now is a black guy named Rico," Matt says. "I'd do anything in the world for him. He's nineteen like me. He knows my whole past and everything. We sit down and talk about it a lot. I feel like I could socialize with anybody and get along with anybody perfectly and that's what I've been doing. I've met a lot of good people that way. I don't care about race or sexual orientation or anything. It feels like a burden's been lifted off my shoulders."

At its peak, Matt's hatred had become complete. "I was getting to the point where I didn't even like white people," he said. So how could a kid with so much hatred—and, with a record of enacting that hatred—find his way out of that tricky forest? What makes him so resolute, so sure that life will be good to him from now on when, from all appearances, there are still so many disadvantages arrayed against him?

"Only God," says Matt. "There's no doubt in my mind because I really wasn't looking to get out of the skinheads. I wasn't really asking for any help. I was really strong into it. There was nothing that could really change my mind. So, do I think He just reached down and got me? Yes. And for the first time that I can remember since I was a little kid, I feel good about my life. I feel right inside."

II

—

Oneless

When it comes to emotional toxins, hatred, real hatred, is in a league of its own. It takes no prisoners; not even its host is spared. Maybe Eric Hoffer, the late philosopher and social critic, put it best. "Passionate hatred can give meaning and purpose to an empty life," he said. I suppose that, in its own way, hatred can be every bit as thrilling and invigorating as love. Either can make you feel incredibly alive. Each can stir the imagination and whisk you away to some fantastical place in your mind. Both love and hate can be feel smart, righteous, and wholly justified.

News archives and law enforcement murder books are full of examples of what hate can do when heavily concentrated and coaxed to a head. But it doesn't take a village. One lost soul is all hate needs to wreak havoc. One captive, like the man in Meridian, Mississippi, who took a twelve-gauge Winchester pump-action shotgun to work at a Lockheed Martin plant on

July 8, 2003, and shot fourteen coworkers, killing five of them before turning the gun on himself. Acquaintances said the man was known for a bad temper that often bulged at the seams. The sheriff called him "an angry man." Several coworkers said he was especially hostile to blacks. Others said any racial animosity the killer held was just part of an all-encompassing, all-consuming hatred. He was, said one man, "mad at the world." And the world won.

Matthew Bishop's abandonment of racial hatred brings to mind a more famous example of heart-cleansing that had occurred nearly forty years prior—the story of Malcolm X, charismatic minister of the Nation of Islam, notorious for adherence to the teachings of black nationalism and, with it, black supremacy. As a spokesperson for the Nation of Islam in the 1960s, Malcolm frequently referred to whites as "blue-eyed devils" and categorically pronounced them as agents and perpetrators of evil, particularly against black people.

Gradually however, Malcolm came to believe that the Nation's principles were a corruption of the faith. Orthodox Islam had begun to take hold of him and thousands of others in the Nation, so that Malcolm helped start a new mosque for Black Muslim traditionalists. In line with this new mind-set, the minister embarked upon the Hajj, a sojourn to Mecca in Saudi Arabia, the cradle of Islam and its holiest city, required of every true Muslim unless finances or health problems prohibit it.

When he returned from his trip to the Middle East and North Africa in May 1964, Malcolm was a changed man. As he noted in his best-selling autobiography, reporters who swarmed him at New York's Kennedy Air Terminal were stunned to hear the minister's new message.

"My pilgrimage broadened my scope," he recalled telling the press. "It blessed me with a new insight. In two weeks in the Holy Land, I saw what I never had seen in thirty-nine years here in America. I saw all races, all colors—blue-eyed blonds to black-skinned Africans—in true brotherhood! In unity! Living as one! Worshipping as one!

"In the past, yes, I have made sweeping indictments of all white people. I never will be guilty of that again, as I know now that some white people are truly sincere, that some truly are capable of being brotherly toward a black man. The true Islam has shown me that a blanket indictment of all white people is as wrong as when whites make blanket indictments against blacks."

The day after that encounter with the media, Malcolm reported, he was in traffic when a white stranger in a nearby car called out to him. "When I looked, he stuck his hand out of his car across at me, grinning. 'Do you mind shaking hands with a white man?' Imagine that!" he wrote. "Just as the light turned green, I told him, 'I don't mind shaking hands with human beings. Are you one?'"

Eight months later, Malcolm had gotten to the point that he not only saw whites as fellow human beings rather than satanic creatures, and as cohorts in the struggle for civil and equal rights rather than saboteurs, but even as acceptable neighbors, friends, classmates, and spouses. In an interview on Canadian television in early 1965, he told the program's host, "When you are dealing with humanity as a family there's no question of integration or intermarriage. It's just one human being marrying another human being or one human being living around and with another human being."

One month later, Malcolm X was gunned down in a Harlem auditorium while spreading the new gospel of a cleansed heart. His final days had been fruitful and inspiring, though he once admitted to Gordon Parks, the famous photographer, artist, and writer, that he had wasted much of his life. "I was hypnotized, pointed in a certain direction and told to march," he told Parks. "Well, I guess a man's entitled to make a fool of himself if he's ready to pay the cost. It cost me twelve years."

As separated as they are by time, race, circumstance, and influence, Malcolm X and Matthew Bishop have, in large measure, a story in common. Each had allowed racial hatred and supremacy to consume about one third of his life. Each found a fraternity of like-minded who embraced, encouraged, and rewarded their vile thinking. Each had an awakening before it was too late. And each recognized that the only power capable of extinguishing the flames of hate and cleaning up the ashes belonged to God.

Aside from this one, there may be no chronicle of Matt's life. He may never be famous, never lead a movement, but his transformation is just as grand an example of grace as Malcolm's. It shows that God can change a heart on an international stage or in a back alley. Whether the call for help comes from a famous orator or a kid who can't quite find the words, God will take the time.

12

—

A Hole in the Soul

On the February night in 1983 when the police nabbed Eddie Velez, he was three days shy of his eighteenth birthday. The bust came toward the end of his senior year in high school.

"I stayed home from school one day, selling this heroin in the projects, only to get arrested," Eddie recalled. Suddenly, he was looking at becoming a man behind bars. But because he was a minor at the time of his arrest, a first offender, and an army reservist, Eddie got off with a little time in jail and probation.

The previous summer, Eddie had signed up for the army reserves in a "spur of the moment" decision, enticed by a friend from the projects who was planning to enlist once he learned he could earn $1,000 for the summer in a local unit. Eddie went to school during the week and did his reserve drills on weekends. In between, he dealt drugs.

"I didn't learn," he said, recalling his near-miss with prison time. "Before you knew it, I was cooking cocaine. Selling it. Smoking it. I was living this double life. A part of me wanted to have ambitions and to do the right thing, but another part of me was sort of enslaved to this street culture."

That street culture had enveloped Eddie on the streets of Jersey City, New Jersey, where he was born in 1965, one of seven children of Puerto Rican immigrants. It was a gritty life in which energies were consumed by eking out a living, or hustling one, and dodging desperados who would scam or take what little you had. There was not much room for the niceties in that place, nor, in some cases, for legalities—not when merely surviving was such a chore.

Worried about the rough neighborhood and their children's exposure to it, Eddie's parents moved the family to Connecticut when Eddie was about ten. They were, of course, looking for a better environment, but they may have only traded addresses. "The way I look at it, we left one hood and went into another," Eddie says.

Chameleon-like, the boy soon took on the pallor of his new environment. His friends were aimless and mischievous; they toyed with assorted dangers, especially with drugs. Eddie followed suit. By the time he was thirteen years old, he was regularly smoking marijuana with his friends. By sixteen, he was snorting cocaine. At seventeen, he was mixing cocaine and heroin. So by the time he was arrested on that winter evening, Eddie Velez had been drugging for four years.

Yet unlike some of his friends, Eddie was not lazy. A part of him craved investiture in the legitimate world, the mainstream where his parents struggled to stay afloat. At nineteen, he got a job with the U.S. Postal Service delivering mail. But at the same time, "I was putting so much cocaine up my nose when work was over that it's a miracle that I'm still here today.

"I had a lot of family in the Bronx, so I was leaving Connecticut to go into the Bronx buying two, three, four, five ounces of cocaine, paying somebody $4,000 to $5,000, and telling myself and my business partner at the time that we're going to make a killing. And before you know it, I was consuming the product. It was just a downward spiral."

Most of the time, Eddie, wily and charming, was able to avoid trouble with the two types that would have finished him off, one way or another: law enforcement and violent street thugs. Despite his regular drug use and dealing, he had only one encounter with police after his first arrest. It happened one night when he was driving back to Connecticut from the Bronx. There were two other guys in the car. And five ounces of cocaine.

"I'm coming down the highway, and the Connecticut state troopers have the highway blocked off. One of my boys says, 'Throw the car in reverse.' I've got a headlight out, so we're expecting to get stopped. Sure enough, we are stopped and the trooper says to me, 'Where are you guys coming from?' I said, 'Well, we're coming from Hartford.' He says, 'How can that be? Hartford's the other way.' I told him that there were actually four of us in the car and we had to drop another guy off first. He said, 'Have you guys been drinking tonight?' At that point, I took out my army reserve card and my postal ID. He said, 'Oh, do you know Danny Trollo?' I said, 'Yeah, that's my boss.' And that was it; he told us to get the headlight fixed and let us roll on.

"That night, my boys said to me, 'Eddie, you're a bad boy. I'm going to give you an eight ball just for you.' And I was like, who's the man, who's the man?"

Having verve as well as nerve, Eddie plowed some of his energy into a hopeful career as a hip-hop artist. He showed some talent as a rapper and for a time seriously explored the possibility of becoming a recording artist. Crack cocaine, the next step on Eddie's drug ladder, put an end to that.

He remembers another trip to Connecticut from the Bronx with a fellow who is now dead, courtesy of a dirty needle.

"Before you knew it, my car broke down. Now, I wasn't paying my insurance. I wasn't getting my vehicle serviced, and I left it on the Major Deegan Expressway, only for them to steal everything. So I had nothing to show for it; I still owed money on the car, but had nothing to show for it. And I ended up going on a cocaine binge for two or three days."

Eddie could feel his health, his future, and his luck draining away.

"I could see that I was going to end up either dead or in the penitentiary. At the time, my sister was going into the U.S. Marine Corps. So I went up to her and said, 'Is the recruiter open today?' That was a Saturday morning in January 1988. I went to the recruiter in my mailman's uniform looking bad. He thought I was there to deliver the mail and I said, 'Look man, I need to get out of here. Where can you send me?' Before you know it, I'm signing the papers."

It wasn't long before Eddie Velez, army private, was in

Germany where he struck, admittedly, a poor figure. He could barely do push-ups. His stamina was low. And although he had given up cocaine, Eddie found another "crutch" in alcohol, which he proceeded to abuse apace. He routinely got drunk, all the while pursuing the hip-hop life in his spare time. Eddie signed a modest record deal with a German label and began working the nightclub circuit in Frankfurt.

While there, he also fell in love. She was a fellow soldier, stunningly beautiful and also of Puerto Rican heritage. After a three-month courtship, the couple wed. Together, they enjoyed the nightlife and indulged in its myriad temptations.

Suddenly, one Sunday, things changed.

Eddie: "I was working in a studio on a project and my wife went to church. I called her from the studio and asked how did the whole church thing go. She said, 'I need to talk to you about that.' Then she told me, 'Well, honey, I got saved today.' And you know what my response was? I asked her, 'Well, why did you do that?' She said they asked if we don't know the Lord and aren't saved to raise our hands and she said she just started crying.

"I went kicking, fighting, and scratching a week or two later when she went to be baptized. And that night they preached from Romans 10:9–10. And I'll never forget how clear those words of Scripture were to me that night because I had grown up Catholic and there are so many requirements in Catholicism. So for me to hear *That if you confess with your mouth the Lord Jesus and shall believe in your heart that God raised Him from the dead, you shall be saved,* I was like, naw; it can't be that easy. So, God was introducing me to His grace. He was letting me know that 'it has nothing to do with your performance, it has everything to do with the free gift that I'm presenting you with today to be my son.'"

By Eddie's account, he and his wife were "with the whole church thing for a few months. I knew how to sing the songs. I knew when to stand or when to sit and I didn't have the pressure to make that walk down there every Sunday because I had already done it. But I wasn't growing in God's word."

Before long—"inevitably," Eddie says—he and his wife began backsliding. They started skipping church and stepped up their partying. Soon, the marriage was in trouble, imperiled by mutual infidelities. The couple stayed together, but not happily.

In the summer of 1993, Eddie and his wife were honorably discharged. The couple and their daughter left Germany and settled in Atlanta, in part because of the southern city's reputation as an up-and-coming music capital. Eddie still had dreams of becoming a rap recording artist.

But a visit to the New Birth Church in Atlanta redirected him. The minister there, Bishop Eddie Long, "was just speaking something out of his mouth that just shot through to my inner man," Eddie says. "And it was like God saying, 'Eddie, I want all of your life. I don't just want you coming to church. I don't just want you and your family joining. I want you to surrender it all to me, including your hip-hop. I remember one other night, man, God was just showing me my life and showing me the things I had been through and the prices I had to pay for them when I walked away from Him. And He finally just showed me that if I didn't give it all to Him, it would cost me my life. So I was like, Lord, I'll rhyme for you."

With Bishop Long's guidance, Eddie got in touch with youth detention centers, community centers, and churches engaged in outreach to the area's many troubled or disoriented youth. He became a sensation as a Christian hip-hop artist.

In 1998, Eddie was named cohost of a new radio program in Atlanta—the *Holy Hip-Hop Show*. Success there eventually led to syndication of the program and then to television appearances. Eventually, Eddie Velez, former drug user and dealer, was a licensed minister.

"Here it is today, more than ten years since we came to Atlanta, and I'm serving one of the most dynamic pastors in the world as his youth director. I'm still married to the wife of my youth almost sixteen years later. We have three beautiful children. God has shown me that all of the drama I went through is so I could relate to these teenagers and this hip-hop culture to let them know that God gives life and gives it abundantly. And that, if you be in Him, you will be a new creation. Not a new church member, not a new parishioner, but a new creation."

It still strikes Eddie as miraculous.

"If you had told me when I was smoking weed at thirteen that one day I would be a believer in the Lord, I would have said you gotta be out of your mind. If you had told me at nineteen that one day I would be a minister of the gospel, I would have been, 'Dude, you stopped at the wrong house.' "

Before his salvation, Eddie had not expected to live past thirty-five, if that long. He knew he was on a hazardous road and, despite his staying that course, much of the time, he says, he was afraid.

"Two things really concerned me when I was out on the

street: going to prison, because I loved my freedom; and dying, because I didn't know where I was going.

"What I would say to the young cat out there who is caught in the midst of this lifestyle right now is that, when you hear the voice of the Lord speaking to you, don't harden your heart to His word that day. Be willing to follow the guidance of His voice.

"God was knocking on my door for a good minute and I was too blind to even understand it. Now that I look back on it, I realize God had sent this person to speak to me and that person to speak to me and I just couldn't grab it. But I'm here to say that if you feel God drawing you, don't be like the little rebellious calf in the rodeo, just give up and let Him take you. You might think your life is caught up in a state of junk and there's no way out, but God is still in the supernaturalness business."

PART THREE

❧

Comfort, Endow, and Hearten

13

—

Something Else About Mary

In her little neighborhood, in the stores and shops she frequented, in the Catholic school where she once worked as a cook, in her tight-knit church in Fresno, California, Mary Williams had always been known for her unfailing cheerfulness. It belied the sorrows that had crept into her life, most notably the death of her only child, a daughter, from brain cancer; the death of her husband; and the loss of a breast to cancer.

Millie Carter lived across the street from Mary. They got to know each other when, as a favor to her neighbor, Millie had watched the house, taken in the mail, and watered the flowers when Mary went to Santa Fe to care for her dying daughter. The arrangement, premised on trust, cemented their relationship, turning the two women into solid and permanent intimates. Mary turned to Millie with all of her confidences, experiences, and ideas. What few relatives she had left were scattered around the country and rarely made contact. Millie and her husband, Pete, were about all she had.

Or so it may have seemed. In truth, Mary had an abiding and functional faith in God that helped her stave off loneliness and self-pity and fill the voids with an upbeat, forward-looking attitude that amused, inspired, and at the same time perplexed people who knew her. Even Millie, a longtime believer herself, found Mary's cheerfulness amazing.

In January 2000 Millie's husband, Pete, died. He and Millie had been married for sixty years and, having had no children, they doted on each other and were virtually inseparable. His absence left a gaping hole in Millie's house, in her days, in her life, in her heart. Naturally, kin and friends worried that grief over her partner's death would endanger Millie's already fragile health. They rushed to her side. Several relatives begged Millie to come and live with them. And for a while, she thought about it.

True to form, Mary shifted her faith and happy mien into high gear, smothering her old friend in affection and optimism, comforting Millie, keeping her busy, and helping her stay focused on the infallibility of God's will. Soon, Millie graciously but unequivocally declined the invitations to move in with her sisters and brothers and nieces and nephews. She was staying put in Fresno.

That was welcome news to Mary, who promptly poured her energies into helping her friend negotiate bereavement and the scary new frontiers of widowhood. The two elderly women kept each other going with laughter and occasional outings.

But soon, another piece of news arrived that might have

shaken loose Mary's storied cheerfulness. The old cancer, the villain that had already taken one of her breasts, had returned and was ruthlessly attacking her body. Shortly after Pete died, Mary's oncologist told her the cancer was moving so quickly and thoroughly that he couldn't promise her more than a month. Millie was horrified.

Mary, however, was not. Though she was saddened by the discovery, her prevailing reaction was the stuff of legend, like an apocrypha created or an experience embellished for the purpose of enhancing the mystique of faith—a talking point for spiritual pitchmen, a fairy tale.

But my own mother can attest to the fact that, in no time, Mary began acting as if she had won the lottery. The sweetness in her voice grew even sweeter, her bright outlook got even brighter. My mother witnessed this firsthand when she called Mary to commiserate soon after learning of the prognosis. "Oh honey, I'm fine," Mary told her. "I've got another month!"

No slouch in the faith department herself, my mother was nonetheless incredulous. "She said it with the joy and excitement of a person who's been told she's cured," Mama recalled. "It was just as pleasant and happy as that."

Mama hadn't simply caught Mary on a good day. And that wasn't the medication talking. "That was just Mary," said Millie. "There was something about her that was just at peace with God—all the time, I don't care what happened."

Mary's doctors were astonished and confounded. They tracked the cancer as it spread from one organ to the next. In short order, it had encamped in her entire body. Yet for nearly a year, Mary showed up for her monthly examinations, and each time, the doctors expected it to be her last visit. Each time, they somberly informed Mary that her time was up. Each time they gave her one more month to live. And, thirty days later, there she would come again, smiling and cheerful as always. "When I would take her to the doctor, he would be amazed," Millie recalled. "He didn't expect to see her anymore."

Mary did not make her visit in January 2001. The cancer had finally completed its destruction. But her best friend can't bring herself to grieve too much or for too long. That wouldn't be the way to commemorate Mary. "God had kept her through it all, kept her mind sound and kept her spirits up," said Millie. "She wasn't the least bit afraid. She talked about death just like we talk about life. All along the way, she was ready. All through everything that had happened. All through her daughter's passing and her husband's passing and the cancer. "Mary was a great and faithful woman," said Millie. "But you know, only God could have made her like that."

14

There Is a Balm

From the way Mabel Mitchell strode into the sanctuary that morning with her head held so high and her eyes so bright and her smile so warm, you would never have known that she was a mother in mourning.

Mabel's fourth-born child had just died. Born in 1955, Bruce joined Mabel and Archie Mitchell's happy, good-looking brood with its flair for music and sport. The Mitchell household was devout and secure, upheld by a strong work ethic—Mabel was a teacher; Archie worked for the railroad—and a powerful spiritual one. Mrs. Mitchell, particularly, was well known and respected as a "church woman," a fixture on the religious scene. "My mother brought me up in the church," she says. "We lived down the alley from the church, so we were there morning, noon, and night. And I believed what the preacher said."

Even though she accepted that God has His own timing,

Mrs. Mitchell also believed that parents were supposed to out-live their children. Alas, not so.

In early childhood, Bruce demonstrated an athletic flair that led him to dabble in and eventually master an array of organized sports—basketball, track and field, football. But it was on the football field that Bruce shone brightest. As he grew into a healthy, hardy, and handsome teenager, his reputation for ath-letic prowess, speed, and skill was traveling far and wide. By his senior year in high school, Bruce Mitchell was a recognized sensation and, accordingly, was courted widely and intensely by a stream of college recruiters with visions of championship tro-phies in their heads.

Among Bruce's suitors was Frank Broyles, the former coach and, by then, athletic director at the University of Arkansas's flagship campus in Fayetteville. The Razorbacks wanted Bruce badly, and Broyles turned on the charm in the Mitchells' living room that night.

Strong-willed and politically alert, Bruce minced no words with Broyles. He didn't want to go to Fayetteville, he said, be-cause too many of his friends and acquaintances had com-plained of racial discrimination and tensions on campus.

Indeed, it had only been a few years since a black player broke the color barrier on the football team, and even though the player was exceptional, Broyles had capitulated to anti-integrationists and kept the kid on the bench much of the time. No wonder, then, that black prospects like Bruce were hesitant about becoming Razorbacks.

But Broyles and several influential team boosters persisted, offering Bruce a full four-year scholarship and a litany of assurances. Finally, the Mitchells' son signed with the team and, with some apprehension, headed for the fertile, clear-skied hills of northwest Arkansas to begin summer workouts with the Razorbacks.

When his freshman year began in earnest that fall, Bruce was already something of a celebrity. The news of his recruitment had spread quickly through Fayetteville's rolling hills and great expectations had latched on. Prospering in both the classroom and on the playing field, Bruce enjoyed a fame of which most kids could only dream. But he was not content to bask in glory. Still on guard against prejudice and discrimination, Bruce also became known for his activism, one time using his popularity to leverage demands that the school's cheerleading squad be integrated. "Bruce and some of his friends got members of the team to sign a petition saying they wanted someone black on the squad," Mrs. Mitchell recalled. "When I read it, it was a little harsh, so I said, 'Let me reword some of this.' She did and that's what they presented to Broyles." The school relented.

Bruce was fast and formidable as the team's star cornerback. Sportswriters from across the nation duly took note, pegging the athlete as one of college football's best. Bruce's record on the field validated predictions that, before long, the pro leagues would come calling. It also explained why coaches and fans were particularly gloomy whenever Bruce was injured and had to sit out a game or two or more.

It was the knee, mainly. Bruce had wrenched, sprained,

and torn it several times and, more than once, it took surgery to get him back on his feet. Each time, his mother was at his side in the hospital and through recovery. Each time, Bruce returned to the field.

The operation in mid-December 1976, however, was different. Because it was during Christmas break, the Mitchells brought their son home to North Little Rock for the surgery. On December 17, Mabel and Archie's wedding anniversary, doctors summoned the couple to the hospital. The whole family went. So did a few friends. Once there, they were informed that blood tests routinely conducted before and after surgery had located abnormal blood cells in Bruce's system. Bruce had leukemia.

In simple terms, leukemia is a cancer of the blood cells. It presents itself as overabundant, malformed, and dysfunctional erythrocytes (red cells), which oxygenate the body's organs and tissues; leukocytes (white cells), which help the body resist infectious and disease-bearing bacteria, viruses, and fungi; and, often, an abnormally low supply of platelets, the cells that create blood clots and control bleeding.

As with many cancers, leukemia's cause is unknown. Its incidence is highest among persons of European descent, and it occurs more often in males than in females.

Of all the new leukemia patients today, about 46 percent can expect to be living five years after diagnosis. In the 1970s, when Bruce Mitchell contracted the disease, the five-year survival rate was 35 percent.

Back then, chemotherapy, radiation, and other systemic

therapies were the conventional treatments for leukemia. Bone marrow transplants were still in the first stages and were not yet widely available. The peripheral stem cell transplant—a procedure involving blood collected from the patient's own veins—was unheard of at the time.

Bruce's parents, siblings, and friends were aghast. They weren't experts on leukemia—not yet—but they knew the disease was incurable and, often, terminal.

Bruce was more perplexed than anything. At first, he dismissed the findings, certain that it was mistaken because only white people get leukemia, or so he thought. Regretfully, the doctors assured Bruce that their diagnosis was accurate.

For the next several days and weeks, Bruce submitted to a battery of tests, medications, and blood transfusions. He got over his initial testiness—thanks, in part to the patience and kindness of Sister Elizabeth Ann, a nun the Mitchells came to know—and he resigned himself to making the most of his treatments and whatever time he had left. "I went [to the hospital] every morning before I went to work and every afternoon after work and stayed late into the night," Mrs. Mitchell recalled. "Bruce and I talked a lot. He said, 'I'm going to die.' We went over the fact that we were all going to die and that when depends on the good Lord. And Bruce accepted that because Sister Elizabeth Ann really helped guide him and us." As if preparing for a major game, Bruce steeled his mind for the long, hard battle ahead.

There were some breaks in the clouds. On one occasion,

the entire Razorback football team showed up at the hospital to donate blood. Frank Broyles had arranged for the trip aboard a private plane, chartered, Mrs. Mitchell says, by a person or persons unknown to this day. The teammates gave so much blood that day that, when Bruce was finally discharged, the hospital had a much-needed reserve.

"When he really realized that he had leukemia and what the results would possibly be, he said, 'You know; I wanted to live a long time. I wanted to be a pro football player, but I know that's out now.' Then he laughed and admitted that he wanted to be a pro so he could make money and buy himself a Cadillac. Bruce always wanted a Cadillac. So, I said, 'When you get out of the hospital, I will buy you a Cadillac.' "

You can hear the happiness as Mabel Mitchell drifts back twenty-five years to the day she had to make good on that promise. It is evident that the memory is pleasing, that she enjoys seeing Bruce again in her mind and remembering his excitement over the new car.

"He called me at work the day he was permitted to come home for just a short visit," Mrs. Mitchell says. "He told me he was discharged and had already called his daddy to come to the hospital to get him. But he wanted me to meet them at the Cadillac place.

"Well, when I called the lady at the credit union I belonged to, she said they were not financing big, luxury cars anymore. So I told her the story. They knew all about it, since the press had covered Bruce's illness and all. So the woman said I should just go on to the dealership and have them call the credit union when I got out there."

Mrs. Mitchell proceeded toward the dealership, gripped by both excitement and anxiety. "I prayed all the way, 'Lord, please help me to do what I promised him,' " she said.

When she arrived, Mrs. Mitchell found her son and husband in the owner's office. Bruce was beaming that bright, handsome smile at her. He pointed excitedly to a shiny new silver Deville. His mother smiled back, of course, but inside she was sinking fast. How could she tell him that the deal might not go through?

She didn't have to. A family friend, a man who had done a lot of business at that same dealership over the years, had intervened on the Mitchells' behalf, explaining to the owner that this was Bruce Mitchell, the Razorback star who had thrilled thousands and brought honor to the state's most venerated sports team, and he was battling cancer for his life and, by Jove, he wanted a Cadillac before he died. For the owner, who had himself lost a son to leukemia years before, that cinched it. He passed the sale papers to the Mitchells to sign. They could have the car at cost. The credit union agreed to finance the entire amount.

Of course Bruce insisted on driving home. Mrs. Mitchell rode with him. Along the way, they stopped for gas. "The station tank was the kind that would beep with every pump," she remembered. "And when Bruce was filling it up, it just kept on beeping. That's when I had to pray again. I thought, how am I going to afford even the gas for this big car? But eventually the beeping stopped and we went on, happy. Bruce dropped me off and went riding around."

Headstrong as always, Bruce announced to his family and

doctors one day that he wanted to go back to school. The hospital staff had come to love their famous young patient and wanted to keep him in their daily care, but they knew him well enough by then to understand that returning to school was something that had to happen. Bruce's primary physician made the arrangements, and soon Bruce was wending his way toward Fayetteville in his new silver car.

Although Bruce would no longer play football, the Mitchell family was still anxious about how he would fare, away from home, away from the doctors and nurses who knew his case so intimately, away from the family so devoted to his survival. At the same time, however, the Mitchells were eager for Bruce to enjoy whatever time remained, so they entrusted a cadre of surrogates—professors, ministers, coaches, friends, and doctors—to look after their beloved and keep them informed. Dr. Merlin Augustine, an administrator at the university, and Reverend Marion Humphrey, an ordained Presbyterian minister, became Bruce's chief confidants, counselors, and caretakers.

Back in Fayetteville, Bruce often felt weak and worn, but his medications kept him going enough to at least attend classes, hang out with friends, and cruise the campus and town in his car. He took a special interest in a professor's book project on the subject of mortality. The project gave each man something he needed—the professor found an expert perspective to complement his clinical studies, and Bruce was gratified by an opportunity to educate, enlighten, and, he hoped, encourage people about life at the terminus. Bruce even sought permission to teach the professor's class on death and dying. And got it.

In the fall of 1977, Bruce's condition worsened and he

seemed to sense his impending demise. A letter he wrote to his parents in early October hinted at this understanding, but the letter's tone is notably devoid of self-pity, resentment, and fear or even regret. Instead, it is a work of selflessness, deep insight, faith, and resolution. Mrs. Mitchell still has the original. It is dated October 4, 1977.

Hello Parents,

I'm doing better now and I can feel myself coming around each day. At first when I got back here, I could hardly walk across campus without getting extremely tired, I mean the headaches and pounding heart. Now I seem to be okay. I missed a couple of exams but they are understanding in letting me make up.

I received a letter from Marion Humphrey when I got back. He told me in the letter he wrote you how he tried to explain to you why I had to "do my own thing." He possibly knows I have a strong disposition of doing for myself and not wanting to cause problems economically or mentally to anyone, especially y'all. That is why I keep telling both of you and others don't worry about me. I know I'm sick or ill and I'm dealing with it my way. I'm not going to huddle in a knot and wait for a miracle drug. I know this is in God's plan and it is helping me to do more for other people.

I want you to understand that I view death as a reward. God has other plans for me, maybe not on this earth, and I feel good. You have maybe noticed me reading all these books on death. Well it was only to give me insight, to feel more secure. Believe me, I'm not afraid of death or

being around it. The soul is relieved of physical pain and
heartaches and the person doesn't want to come back.

I'll end up by saying that I'm trying to work out
something with [the University of Arkansas at Little Rock]
to come back home in January, but still be enrolled and
take a course up here so I can have U of A on my diploma.
I'll let you know more about it as I find out more. It's
costing too much money for y'all to have me up and down
the highway every weekend and I realize that.

See you next weekend, will call Sunday.

Love you,
Bruce

Not long after that letter arrived, Dr. Augustine and Reverend Humphrey informed the Mitchells that their son needed to come home. Humphrey told the family he would drive the Cadillac back because Bruce was too weak to make the long ride and would need to fly home. Humphrey would also bring as many of Bruce's belongings as would fit in the car, he said.

"Well, we knew what that meant," says Mrs. Mitchell. "So I said, 'Go ahead and make the arrangements and we'll pay whatever we have to.'" A day or two later, Bruce arrived by private plane. "We met them at the airport and that's when we found out we didn't have to pay for the plane," Mrs. Mitchell said. "We were going to pay the pilot at least, but he wouldn't accept anything. I tell you, they were good to my child."

• • •

Normally, mid-October would find Bruce Mitchell suited up in pads, helmet, cleats, darting and barreling on the gridiron, defending his goal. He had spent most of the autumns of his life that way. But in October of 1977, Bruce was in a hospital bed, clinging to his young life as the cancer went about its deadly business. Warned by doctors that Bruce was in extremis, family and friends drew near. Mrs. Mitchell stayed by her son's side day and night, talking to him, reading to him, as Sister Elizabeth Ann had encouraged her to do.

Despite his deteriorating state, Bruce, says his mother, was serene and often alert. He even helped his mother write the speech she was scheduled to give later that month as keynote speaker for the annual "Women's Day" service at Shiloh Baptist, a neighboring church.

"I would take my pad and pen and write in the hospital, right there next to him," she said. "Then I would read what I had written to him. He was really listening. Sometimes he would say, 'Mama, don't say that, say so-and-so instead' and I would change it. Sometimes I would take a popular song and kind of write my own words around it. And Bruce would say, don't use that song; use this song. He was very helpful."

On Friday, October 21, Bruce's doctor told the family that it was just a matter of time. Other relatives and friends rushed to the hospital to hold vigil. That evening, they retired to the Mitchell home with plans to return the next day.

On Saturday morning, Mrs. Mitchell noticed that Bruce's breathing had become labored and heavy so she summoned a nurse. "When I looked up, Sister Elizabeth Ann was there along with the doctor. He said to me, 'You need to call the children,' so that's what we did. We were all gathered around him when we found out he was in a coma. He never did wake up." That evening, Bruce Mitchell slipped away. He was twenty-two years old.

Word of Bruce's death raced through the community like wildfire. Phones were ringing all over town; reporters were on the move; friends, neighbors, coworkers, business leaders, and church members appeared at the Mitchells' door with food, flowers, and heartfelt condolences. Shirley Davis, the chairwoman of the Women's Day committee at Shiloh, called to offer her sympathies and to assure Mrs. Mitchell that the congregation did not expect her to carry through with her speaking commitment under the circumstances, but would find a substitute speaker, not to worry.

"I said, 'Shirley, I want to still do it because Bruce helped me write this speech and he would want me to go on with it,'" Mrs. Mitchell recalled. "In fact, several people called to make sure I still wanted to do it and I did."

And so, that Sunday morning, she set out for Shiloh right on schedule. When she walked in, upright and composed, resplendent in suit and hat, an audible gasp wafted through the sanctuary. Bruce had died only the night before, a matter of hours, and yet there she was, ready to extol God's goodness. And what a speech it was.

As I sat there, stricken by Mabel Mitchell's strength and courage and the power of her words, I could not believe it all. Judging from the whispers around me, neither could most of the congregation. "Only God," came a woman's voice from behind me. Only God indeed.

A quarter of a century has passed since Bruce Mitchell walked off the field. Like anyone who leaves too soon, Bruce left a bounty of happy memories and a proud reputation with which to recall his life. But, unlike most twenty-two-year-olds, he also left a legacy.

At the University of Arkansas at Fayetteville, Dr. Augustine established a memorial fund in his name that helps students who otherwise wouldn't have the money to go home during holidays or at year's end. The Little Rock Razorback Club, an organization of fans and boosters, presents the Bruce Mitchell Award at their annual banquet each year. Every year at his old high school, student athletes and their parents relish the presentation of the Bruce Mitchell Award to the school's outstanding athlete. The Arkansas Children's Hospital and St. Vincent Medical Center have both commemorated Bruce.

In addition to trophies, plaques, and newspaper clippings galore, the Mitchells also have another reminder of their son's latter years. In 1978, the year Bruce would have graduated from the University of Arkansas, officials hosted the family at a special luncheon and presented Bruce's diploma.

Meanwhile, the Mitchell family has continued to prosper under the spiritual faith that had rescued Bruce from the bowels of despair and had imbued his loved ones with uncommon courage and peace of mind.

"Right now in our home church, every member of my

family that lives here in town belongs to our church. Bruce had a son, Brent, and he joined the church years ago. He's grown now, married, has a child. His wife came and joined the church, too. Every one of my children and my grandchildren are in the church and working in the church. I mean, really working. To me, that's a blessing."

If you ask Mabel Mitchell how she has managed to carry on without bitterness or regret, without feeling cheated of a son who brought so much joy and pride to her life, she is unhesitating.

"I have a saying," she explains. "If God puts you to it, He'll bring you through it. I am a witness for that."

Not long ago, Mrs. Mitchell, now divorced, was being honored for her long service to the community. One of the speakers mentioned Bruce's death as an example of the tribulations she has weathered over the years. Imagine the heartbreak and loneliness, he had said.

"When it was over, I went up to him and thanked him, but I said, I have to disagree with some of what you said," she says. "I had to tell him that I'm not lonely. I've got God in my house with me."

15

—

Peace Like a River

It wasn't a disease that sneaked up and took Darrell Scott's daughter away in 1999 when she was only seventeen years old. It was a fellow student. Two of them in fact. Rachel Scott was one of the thirteen students and teachers gunned down at Columbine High School in Littleton, Colorado, by fellow students Dylan Klebold and Eric Harris. The massacre at Columbine shook the nation and the world. Even in an era of epidemic violence, a schoolhouse slaughter—committed by young people, no less—was unheard of.

About a month before she died in April, Rachel had written an essay entitled "My Ethics, My Codes of Life." As her father explained to CNN in October of 2002, Rachel had written "about compassion, kindness, reaching out to people who weren't being reached out to. In her diary she wrote and she prayed, God help me to reach people who aren't being reached."

Darrell Scott took his daughter's essay as a last will and testament. Accordingly, when he heard that a certain prison inmate had repented of his sins and had a change of heart, Scott made a point of meeting the man, hoping to encourage him in his lowly estate.

But Scott's new acquaintance was no run-of-the-mill prisoner. He was David Berkowitz, convicted serial killer, the notorious "Son of Sam," the man who had terrorized New York City in the summer of 1977 with random, scattered murders of unsuspecting strangers. By the time police got their hands on Berkowitz, he had killed six people.

"I certainly don't condone the things he did," Scott told the network, speaking of Berkowitz. "He did horrible things when he was twenty-three years old . . . but thank God people can change and that over a period of time, hearts can change. It doesn't mean that he shouldn't be punished for what he did. . . ."

Did that mean he had pardoned Klebold and Harris? No, said Scott, but he did not want to commemorate his daughter's death with a sour heart. "I meet with families of victims all the time and I watch people who don't forgive and many times they become bitter and angry. It victimizes them over and over again."

How did Darrell Scott manage his own grief, how did he stave off bitterness, how did he resist the temptation to seek revenge that would only seem normal under the tragic circumstances?

"There is a God," he said. "Through His strength and grace."

16

They That Wait

First, a brief review of our assembly.

In adults, the spinal cord is about eighteen inches long. The bony but flexible vertebra protect the cord and its bundle of nerves. The vertebra are divided into four segments: cervical (the neck); thoracic (the chest); lumbar (between the ribs and pelvis); and sacral (the pelvis and hips). Damage to the vertebra threatens the cord and that, in turn, puts speech, motor skills, and sensation at risk.

Every year in the United States, approximately eleven thousand people suffer a spinal cord injury. The extent of their injuries depends on what segment of the cord was damaged. Generally, the higher up the cord, the more body parts are affected. Whether the injury is permanent or temporary depends on whether the damage to the cord is "complete" or "incomplete."

For Jason Mathis, my nephew, the injury occurred in the fifth and sixth cervical vertebra. They were complete.

From the very beginning, Jason was a most agreeable child— healthy and strong, quick to smile or chuckle, easygoing, unde- manding. Although his father was absent, Jason was such a joy to his mother that, for the first couple of years, it seemed, she never put him down. They lived with her parents and Granny and Granddaddy promptly fell head over heels for the chubby little baby who was, after a handful of girls, their first grandson.

Growing up with Jason as a cousin and playmate, my own children adored him. His lightheartedness and quiet but fun- loving demeanor appealed to them. They also liked his sense of mischief and engaged in several childish exploits with him. Once, when Jason was visiting my home, I discovered that my son, Joseph, who was then four years old, had torn a little plastic door on a brand spanking new TV off its hinges. When I asked him whatever had possessed him, he said Jason told him to do it. Since Jason was about seven at the time and old enough to know better—as was Joseph, actually—I confronted him with Joseph's story. But rather than hem and haw, Jason confessed immediately and said, ruefully, "I'm sorry, Aunt Deb." He was so forthcoming, sweet, and sincere about it that I dismissed the matter with a simple "Don't do anything like that again" and joked that the TV looked more high tech without the little plas- tic door anyway. I fell in love with Jason anew.

What he meant to his mother and grandparents—the peo- ple who saw him day in and day out—cannot be measured. He never caused them any trouble to speak of but studiously avoided the trap that had ensnared so many of his friends and classmates—the drug-gang-dropout trap. By the end of his senior year in high school, Jason was a tall and handsome young man with college on his mind.

In order to stay close to family, Jason enrolled in a mid-sized state university about thirty miles from home. He would live on campus but could get to his mother and grandparents quickly if needed. Jason thrived in the school's buzzing social atmosphere, but his academic work in the school of mass communications was mediocre. Like many young people away from home for the first time, Jason failed to find that balance between work and play.

Then Genesis came along. Pretty, petite, and gentle, she caught Jason's eye, he caught hers, and before long, they were a couple. But Genesis was more than Jason's girlfriend, she was also his muse. She could be playful and pleasant, but the young woman was serious about schoolwork. Through gentle persuasion and by example, she inspired Jason to rededicate himself to his studies and to make education, not socializing, his priority in college. Not only did his grades rebound, but his self-confidence also soared. He began seeing his future self as a news photographer, like his beloved uncle Chris. In addition to an exciting and portable career, the news business would provide Jason with a good salary that he planned to share with his mother and grandparents as reward for their long years of sacrifice with creature comforts, travel, and tender loving care.

To keep the work–play balance on an even keel, Jason turned to a fraternity as his main source of fun, entertainment, and camaraderie. He pledged Alpha Phi Alpha, one of the oldest and most respected black fraternities of all the Greek societies. It is renown for its scholars, its dignity, and its commitment to public service. Many of the country's most accomplished black men are Alphas.

Normally cool as a cucumber, Jason could not hold down his pride and excitement when he finally completed the sometimes grueling and humbling demands of probation and finally "crossed over" to become, officially and evermore, an Alpha. To celebrate the achievement, as well as the end of another school year, Jason and several other young Alphas set off on a weekend trip to Memphis, Tennessee, about 165 miles northeast of the college campus. The fraternity picked up the tab.

After a full day of fun and frivolity, the fellows considered staying in Memphis overnight, but money was tight. Besides, they would need time to get back to school, gather some things and scatter to various parts of the state for Mother's Day that Sunday.

So in the wee hours of a Saturday morning, the young men set out—fourteen of them in a large van—with one of the friends behind the wheel.

The stretch of highway between Memphis and Conway, Arkansas, is long, straight, and boring. For much of the way, the road is lined on either side by farmland—acres and acres of rich delta soil nourishing soybeans and cotton or, in some places, catfish ponds. It makes for tranquil scenery, but the sameness can have a lulling effect on the traveler with miles to go, especially in the middle of the night.

Sure enough, several of the passengers fell asleep. Jason, seated on the van's third bench, pulled his orange T-shirt over his head and rested his head on the back of the second row. The next thing he remembers was hearing someone shout "Watch out!" Jason tried to pull the T-shirt down so he could see what was happening, but it was too late.

Jason does not remember the accident. He does not remember shooting down the median for 440 feet before veering back onto the interstate. He does not remember the van leaving the road and overturning five times. He does not remember being thrown from the vehicle into the sidelong grass. "The next time I woke up I was on the ground," Jason says. "All these people were standing around, talking about 'don't move,' when in fact I couldn't move. I couldn't feel anything. The next thing I remember was halfway waking up in the hospital, lying on this board. I was crying for them to get me off of it but they said, 'Stay right there because you might have spinal cord injuries.' But for the most part, I was out of it."

Jason lay in the Elvis Presley Regional Trauma Center in Memphis for nearly three weeks. It was there, during emergency surgery, that doctors discovered the severed nerves in his spinal column. When the medical team explained the implications of complete injuries to the C-5 and C-6 vertebra, that Jason could be permanently paralyzed from his shoulders down, the family fell to pieces with grief.

"In Memphis, I really didn't know what was happening because I was so drugged up," Jason recalled. "Everybody was coming in and out, and I knew it was bad, but I can't say that I was really aware of what was going on." He didn't know then, for example, that the crash had killed two of his friends—Brandon Davis and Gavin Morgan, both twenty years old. It would be a couple of weeks before he learned that tragic news and that another friend in the van, Dorsey Watson, had succumbed to his injuries there in the same trauma center where Jason fought for his life.

Soon after discharge from the Memphis hospital, Jason was admitted to the Shepherd Center in Atlanta, one of the nation's premier rehabilitation centers for patients with neurological injuries and disorders and the largest catastrophic care center in America. Founded in 1975 by Alana and Harold Shepherd, whose son was paralyzed in a surfing accident two years before, the center takes a holistic approach to therapy, replete with family counseling. "Shepherd really explains your body to you," Jason said. "I had classes, physical therapy, and lots of meetings with the doctors and caseworkers. I was there for two or three months and it really helped a lot."

But it was also at Shepherd that, as Jason puts it, "the drugs started wearing off and it really hit me that I may not walk again." Up until that point, Jason had expected his mobility to return as the swelling decreased and his body got back to normal. The possibility—no, probability—that he would be a quadriplegic for life, he says, nearly finished him off.

"If you don't have a strong mind, it will break you," Jason says. "That's why it's really important that people stick around you."

For the first several months, friends were everywhere.

They called and e-mailed him. They dropped by for long visits; a few took him for rides. But, in time, the visits and calls dwindled, his relationship with Genesis ended, and Jason became an unwilling homebody, reliant on his mother, grandparents, and other relatives to serve as his hands and feet. But then there was also a young man named Tony, a childhood friend. He has been faithful and unfailing, a veritable brother to Jason and, as some would swear, a possible angel, too. "I was going to church all of my life, but in college, staying out late, I really didn't go to church that much. But once I got back home after the accident and Tony started coming around, I started going to church with him. Tony brought me a Bible, and every day he read verses and explained to me what they mean. When we went to church, I found myself enjoying it more than I thought, so we went more than on just Sunday."

And that's where Jason reconnected with the best friend he's ever had, a friend who shows up . . . well, religiously.

"Throughout this process, I've come closer to the Lord," Jason says. "I talk to Him every night and every day. I think of everything He's done for me. I ask Him to keep looking out for me. It's amazing the stuff He does. He made me realize that all this happened for a reason. It may not be for me, it may be for someone else. But I know God didn't just sit back and let this happen for nothing. That's not how He works."

If you couldn't see him in that wheelchair, if you could only hear him, you'd have no way of knowing that Jason Mathis is disabled. No way of knowing that he is deprived of some of the simplest, everyday pleasures—embracing his mother, fixing a bowl of ice cream, tossing a football with his friends, bouncing baby cousins on his knee, putting himself to bed.

His voice is relaxed and pleasant, he still has a ready laugh, and there is not a whit of bitterness about him. Indeed, Jason is remarkably upbeat—a function of his faith in a God whom he knows might, at any minute, fire up those nerves again. Jason knows that hope, the anticipation that any tomorrow or every tomorrow may be the magic day, is a gift from on high.

"God could just walk up and heal me, but He might do it through somebody else's hands," says Jason. "All of this medicine coming out, all the stem cell research and everything, that's Him, too."

Jason insists that, every now and then, he feels a tingle in his legs. Sometimes it's more like a throb. His doctors may not be sure what to make of it—the injuries were so severe, after all. But Jason is drenched in hope.

"I actually know I'm going to walk again, so I'm not worrying about it, I'm just waiting on Him."

As a child of God, my third toughest challenge has been to explain to skeptics and nonbelievers why God, who is purported to be all good and merciful, allows bad, even awful, things to happen to people who are, from all appearances, undeserving of such misfortune, if not altogether innocent, as in the case of children. The second toughest challenge comes in trying to explain it to myself. The first and foremost challenge is to accept tragedy and disappointment as part of the master plan, as God's will, even when, by any human construct, it seems unfair, maybe even cruel.

Over the years, I've made several vain attempts at unraveling the mystery of why, as one author once put it, "bad things happen to good people." The concept that tragedy is a conduit for a greater lesson or long-term blessing, either for the afflicted person or someone near, is one of the more popular explanations. Then there's the argument that God imposes misfortunes upon us to "test" our faithfulness to Him, which, for me, sounds like a setup and not something becoming a benevolent, divine power. Tragedy and misfortune may certainly test that faith, but I don't buy that it's the purpose behind the incident. Might such things make us more faithful? Yes. But as a diagnostic tool? I don't believe it. Besides, He knows.

Now in my fiftieth year, I've gotten comfortable with the only conclusion that makes sense: Only God knows why such things happen. That answer will not help me win a debate with agnostics or atheists and it's not likely to create the impression that I have thought deeply about this. But that would be wrong. I think about it all the time, especially as the days unfold their tragic tales—a child killed by a parent, a sickly man beaten to death by an irate motorist, a whole family vanquished by fire, a pregnant woman killed and dumped into a bay.

But I understand now that, try as I might, I do not have the capacity to understand some things and to reconcile them with what I know about God's goodness. Yet I am so sure of His goodness that I have learned to trust His decisions without needing to know why. I understand that God makes some things happen and allows others to happen. Whether it's hands-on or hands-off depends, I believe, on whether we have chosen to follow His plan or our own.

I consider that childlike trust a blessing because it has been there when reason, fairness, and justice—humankind's measuring sticks for righteousness—have failed. That trust has shepherded me through many a storm—times when the shock, the grief, the fear, and the pain were so powerful that, had I not believed that God was in control, I would have gone off the deep end. Time and again, He put my mind and heart at peace when circumstances defied it.

PART FOUR

❧

Inspire, Edify,

Propel, and Enlighten

17

We Interrupt This Program

How do I describe the inspiring or directive voice of God? First, I guess I'd have to say there is no pattern to it. It may wake you up or stop you in your tracks, but not necessarily. It can be urgent, but not always. It might be recurring, redundant, insistent, but maybe not. And it doesn't always come in complete sentences or finished thoughts. It may be just a word. Actually, it's not really a voice at all. Oprah Winfrey calls it a "whisper." That's more like it, but it's not exactly that either. When God speaks to a heart, it is similar to conscience, imagination, and intuition, but more like an understanding, a sense of something. But somehow you are made aware that the thought didn't come from you. And, at least eventually, you are made aware of whence it did come.

On the third Saturday in September of 1994, the CBS network premiered a show called *Touched by an Angel*. In that inaugural episode, a novice angel named Monica takes her first assignment as an earthly guardian. She meets her new charge on a bus. David is a sorrowful young boy. As the bus moves on and the two develop a friendship, Monica learns that the root of David's unhappiness was the death of his mother and baby sister. David's father hires Monica as a live-in nanny and it is in the course of that work that she encounters the Angel of Death who explains that the baby girl had died in infancy but that the mother is alive, working as a waitress in a seedy cafe and wrestling with guilt over the death of her daughter. Monica tries to persuade the mother to return to her husband and son, but to no avail. When Monica returns without the mother, the boy is heartbroken. Because she botched her first assignment, Monica gets into trouble with her mentor, a veteran angel named Tess, and prays for forgiveness. But just as David is being consoled over the news that his mother will not be coming back, the mother arrives. The family is happily reunited.

Reviewers tore the new show to shreds. They called it sappy, simplistic, and predictable. Hounded by critics, *Touched by an Angel* seemed headed for cancellation almost from the start. After all, this was a year for comedies. In 1994, seven of the ten most popular TV shows were designed to make people laugh, usually with bawdy, risqué shtick. *60 Minutes, Murder, She Wrote,* and *Monday Night Football* rounded out the top ten.

Regardless of the put-downs and doomsaying by critics and the television community at large—and even some who welcomed a show about spirituality yet accused *Touched* of being shallow—the viewing public flocked to the show. By 1997 it ranked third in the all-important Nielsen ratings by which TV advertising rates rise and fall. By its fifth year, *Touched* was number two on the charts, drawing nearly twenty million viewers each week. The show led the field in its sixth year.

Many people believed the show thrived because God was pleased by its message, overruled skeptics, and turned the show into a solid, albeit improbable, hit. Whether God dabbles in television ratings is an issue that can only lead to arguments, since it is an unanswerable question and would no doubt strike some as preposterous. It is inarguable, however, that, for whatever reason, *Touched* struck a chord. For that, the show's executive producer and occasional writer, Martha Williamson, credited the simple and recurring message that rounds out every episode: God is real.

As Williamson once explained in an article for *Written By,* a magazine for television and film writers, "You cannot have an angel walk away at the end of a show and say, 'Well, you know, it's up to you whether you believe in God or not. He seems okay to me.' You must have an angel who says, 'God exists. God loves you. God wants to be part of your life.' If there's anything left up in the air at the end of an episode, it's 'Will that person embrace that?' It's different from any drama that deals with anything supernatural in that we are dealing every week with something generally accepted to be true: God exists."

The inspiration for the show is, itself, a story of faith. Williamson talked about it in an interview on *Fox News Sunday* in the fall of 1999, as *Touched* was entering its fifth season.

"You know, people are going to laugh and point and say, 'Oh, my God, look at this woman; she is hearing voices.' No, there's something different," she said. "You have to stop and listen to what's going on in the universe. And it sounds so New Agey, but I listen to God. I said to God, 'Look, get rid of what's going on in my head and get rid of what's going on in my heart, and place something in there.' And I've never ever had a script that was great that didn't come from something that I couldn't point—that . . . how do I put this? Well, it is so wonderful, you know, when you talk about God. Something happens inside that you know you didn't formulate in your brain. We were writing a Rosa Parks episode and I wrote all this stuff and then I went back and said, where did that come from? And you know it didn't come from you."

18

Falling Up

Defying and ignoring the voice, or, alternatively, deceiving ourselves about its source, its admonitions, or its instructions can be a costly mistake, albeit not always a measurable one. Who knows what time and opportunities we've lost, what blessings we've forfeited or delayed, because we blocked out that voice or reasoned it away?

Doing that may even be dangerous. We ignore God at our peril. He may let us get away with disregarding the voice for a while, but eventually He will get our attention—the hard way, if that's what it takes. He is the boss, after all.

Can I get a witness? Let me turn to Al Green, the legendary soul singer who brought us "Let's Stay Together," "Love and Happiness," "Still in Love with You," and "Tired of Being Alone," to name but a few of his big hits. Green grew up in Forrest City, Arkansas—a farm town whose nearest big city was Memphis, Tennessee, a blues and rock 'n' roll nursery that would put, among others, Elvis Presley and Isaac Hayes on the map. As a kid, Al sang with the Green Brothers, a gospel group that enjoyed modest success on the southern gospel circuit in the 1950s. Al was expelled from the group when his manager-father caught him listening to rhythm and blues sensation Jackie Wilson's sexy, street-hip music. In high school, Green formed his own group—Al Green and the Creations, and, later, the Soul Mates.

Al was twenty-three years old when he met Willie Mitchell, who ran the Memphis-based Hi Records label. Mitchell, a Mississippi-born trumpet player who had proven his chops as a touring performer, was a respected fixture on the Memphis music scene but was looking for a breakthrough. Mitchell gambled that Green's soulful voice, with its natural blues, gospel and jazz tones, would be a perfect match for the organ and horn-based, drum-driven arrangements for which Hi Records was becoming known.

The gamble paid off quickly. Under Mitchell's tutelage and production, Green's singing career soared. The artist collected hits like they were wildflowers. But four years into his rocketing fame, trouble struck. Green's girlfriend, in a fit of depression and distress, poured hot grits on him, scalding the singer. Then she killed herself.

As Green saw it, the tragedy was a signal from God that it was time to abandon the R&B genre and recommit his acclaimed talents to spiritual works. Green was shaken by the revelation, but not stirred. He turned off the voice and continued to make music that emphasized sensual, and sexual, delights.

My husband and I met Willie Mitchell in late 1979 while visiting a friend who, at the time, was dating Mitchell's daughter. Generously, the great hit-maker spent an entire evening with us, hosting us in his palatial home in the heart of the city, regaling us with stories about his various adventures on the music trail, and late into the evening, taking us on a tour of his famous studio. As if that were not enough, Mitchell gave us another treat: a private listen to Al Green's very first studio session with Hi Records.

We didn't know it then, but around the same time that we were listening to him at the start of his transformation from wannabe to legend, Al Green was going through another change. During a concert in Cincinnati, he had taken a fall from the stage. Though his injuries were not grave, they did require two weeks of hospitalization. As far as Green was concerned, there was no denying the message that time. God had spoken loudly and clearly. The secular stuff would have to go.

At the end of 1979, Al Green announced his retirement from the R&B scene. He found a new calling as a Pentecostal minister and, returning to his roots, embarked upon a career as a gospel singer. Mitchell produced the Reverend Al Green's first spiritual album, *He Is the Light*. There would be others. And by 1995, when Green was inducted into the Rock and Roll Hall of Fame, he had collected eight Grammy awards, all for his gospel recordings. Despite busting the charts over and over again during his R&B career, Green had never won a Grammy for any of that music.

In a 2001 interview with an online music magazine based in Ireland, where he was on tour, Green provided a glimpse of his conversion and the continuing struggle to stay on track, in tune with God.

"I wouldn't say I regret my past," he said. "I would say to anyone in that situation to work hard, have fun, enjoy yourselves, but always realize that someday you will need to get in touch with yourself. You will need to think about your life, think about how you could be using your gifts, and think about where your gifts came from. You know, son, I'm glad I went through everything I did. The love of a woman is a great thing, but the love of God is greater. For twenty-three years now, though, I've been living with the love of God solely. When I play live, and all the women are tempting me down the wrong path, I think maybe my spirituality might be connecting with them. That they might go home, having been entertained and moved, but also maybe with a little more spirituality in their lives."

19

Safety in the Lions' Den

Dangerous, troublemaking street gangs are nearly as old as America herself. The country's early sociology is bound up in the rivalries of ethnic and neighborhood confederates whose shenanigans were routinely mischievous and sometimes dangerous.

But in the 1980s, the combination of illegal drugs, readily accessible guns, the glorification of violence, and pernicious poverty gave gang life a new and deadlier edge. Now, the gangs no longer confined their targets to rival gangsters or their sympathizers and abettors, but took it to whole households and neighborhoods, often firing indiscriminately in what became known as the drive-by shooting. In addition to thousands of young gang members, scores of innocent men, women, children, and infants succumbed to the crossfire.

At first, organized, underground street gangs were a big-city phenomenon. But by the start of the 1990s, every major city in America had a "gang problem." By the end of the decade, many small towns and rural communities did, too.

Little Rock, Arkansas—my hometown—had a population of just under 200,000 in 1993, the year the cable giant HBO aired a documentary about gang violence under the aegis of its award-winning *America Undercover* series. The Arkansas capital might have seemed an unlikely choice for a program about a crisis with nationwide implications. But the city was a hotbed of gang activity. In the 1990s law enforcement officials had identified fifty distinct street gangs with memberships in the thousands, and growing. The homicide count was in record-breaking territory, with increasing numbers of young victims— the yield of raging violence in the streets, the quarry of a horrendous competition for control and deference.

Sadly, HBO had come to the right place. It titled the program *Gang War: Bangin' in Little Rock.*

Destined to become a classic, *Bangin' in Little Rock* pulled the covers off a world no more than a few minutes' drive away for some people—and only around the corner for others—but to most, a foreign place. What little most people knew of gangs had come from a patchwork of movie scenes, news accounts, rap lyrics, and statistics. This faint familiarity, this sketchy understanding of gang life was the logical result of concerted efforts to cordon off gangs and their territory from mainstream society. But as gang activity spilled over the walls and became a malignant and widespread menace, society turned up the heat with harsh, new, punitive measures.

Fearful and outraged, the country resorted to knee-jerk solutions: mandatory minimum sentencing; formulaic punish-

ments like "Three Strikes and You're Out" laws; and a shame-less double standard under which possessing and selling rock cocaine (the cheap form called "crack") resulted in multiples of the jail time imposed on possessors or dealers of powder co-caine (the "yuppies' choice"). Soon, any public curiosity about gangs and their culture of revenge, intimidation, drugs, and turf control was manifestly overwhelmed by trepidation and spite.

People in law enforcement—the first responders to crime scenes—began burning out. The endless encounters with dead bodies, with bereaved mothers and fathers, wore them down. They either quit the job, got themselves reassigned, or allowed their sensibilities to "numb out" in order to stay on the case. Many lost interest in the "whys" of gang life. What mattered to them were the tremors and aftershocks that were shaking soci-ety to its core.

As their guide and consultant through the dangerous, tur-bulent gang zones, the HBO crew chose Steve Nawojczyk, the longtime coroner of Pulaski County, which encompassed sev-eral of these zones. Having run the state crime lab for two years and then served as coroner for ten, Steve Nawojczyk knew the body count firsthand. He had seen them all: the gangbanger gunned down on a street corner; the grandmother felled in her garden during a drive-by; the suspected "snitch" rendered un-recognizable by gunshots to the face; the baby with scraps from her receiving blanket lodged in her back.

Nawojczyk did his job promptly and efficiently, but not dispassionately. Try as he might, he could not "numb out." In his own way, the gangs were killing him, too, slowly and invis-

ibly. When it got to be too much, he put his investigative skills to work to track down the "why" and get to the bottom of an epidemic that was only worsening with time.

In between responses to death scenes, Nawojczyk started hanging out with gang members "to learn why kids were killing one another over something as simple as a stare down."

In short order, Nawojczyk became a fixture in the danger zone. Though some gang members were convinced that he was a narc and a spy for police, others warmed up to him. Even if they didn't trust him, they respected his fearlessness in strolling into areas that most people would not even drive near. In the process, he came to know the culture. He became an expert in their slang, their slogans, their symbols, their code. He learned to read and interpret their graffiti and their hand signals. He understood the significance of certain colors, tattoos, body branding, and hairstyles.

"Every kid I met on the street was part of the Five-H Club," Nawojczyk said. "Helpless, hopeless, homeless, hungry, hugless. The gangs step in to fill that void. They give the kids identity, recognition, belonging, discipline, love, and respect."

No small number of people thought Nawojczyk was nuts. Some wrote him off as a misguided do-gooder, a crusader with good intentions but flawed methodology. Others criticized him for "negotiating with terrorists," accusing him of appeasing unrepentant, hell-bent criminals. Worse, his appeals to lawmakers and policymakers to focus as much on gang prevention as on gang control were largely ignored.

Setbacks notwithstanding, Nawojczyk persisted, hungry for insight and for answers. He widened his network of friends

and sources in the gang world. On the solution side, his allies were limited to a few intrepid social service organizations and some church groups that, like the coroner, were dedicated to the arduous and often frustrating labors of prevention and rescue. For the most part, the larger community turned its back to the crisis, lending little more than scorn and a reliance on law enforcement and the courts to the remedial campaign.

After a while, Nawojczyk began seeing his gang acquaintances at work. More and more, the corpses were familiar. They were kids he had known and counseled. He knew their mothers, their baby brothers and sisters, their neglected talents. He couldn't take it anymore.

Although he had been elected and reelected coroner six times and was certain to be again if that's what he wanted, sometime before the 1994 election season rolled around, Nawojczyk decided to leave the post. He knew it was time to plunge full-time into working with the gangs, to try to stop the violence and uplift the kids entangled in the web of violence and premature death. The voice assured him it was the thing to do. But how would he earn a living and how would he organize a campaign to cure the gang problem?

"I had absolutely no idea what I was going to do," Nawojczyk admits. "That's where there may have been some divine intervention in the form of the notoriety the HBO show gave me. Even though my own community didn't seem to care what I had to say, it became evident lots of others did."

After *Gang War: Bangin' in Little Rock* aired, Nawojczyk's

phone started ringing and wouldn't stop. He was getting speaking invitations from all over the country—people who wanted to learn what he had learned and to hear his plainspoken message about what a gang-ridden community could, and should, do. Lectures, community meetings, and mediation efforts took him to thirty-five states. He consulted city governments, church groups, police departments, and gang intervention organizations. Along the way, he watched a number of "bangers" abandon the gang life and return to school, join the workforce, reconcile with their families, and in a number of instances take up the cause of gang prevention themselves. Nawojczyk was most gratified by the former bangers who became tutors and mentors—positive role models—in their community. The transformed who became reformers brought a credibility and accessibility to the effort that not even a devoted activist like Steve could bring.

"As the years wore on, so did I," said Nawojczyk. "I mean, I was wearing out. Traveling across the country wore me down." Still, the voice—that sense, that understanding that has no name—propelled him forward. Not long after acknowledging his exhaustion, the peripatetic crusader was out on a walk for relaxation. His route took him past the home of Patrick Henry Hays, mayor of North Little Rock, the capital's sister city just across the river. "He was out working in his yard and we struck up a chat," Nawojczyk recalled. "He told me to call him if I ever thought about a 'real job' again. I did and he hired me."

Nawojczyk was assigned to monitor a residential drug treatment program for pregnant women in one of the city's poorest housing projects. "This program gets at the root of the problem—intervening to prevent children from taking a disastrous course," said the incurable optimist. As director of North Little Rock's Juvenile Services, Nawojczyk now has the institutional power he needs to put muscle behind his ideas for eradicating the infamous Five-H Club. It not only saves young lives from being wasted and threatened, he says, but it makes the community safer and more caring. Now he helps shape the policy that shapes young lives, though he still applies the personal touch, as in the case of Matthew Bishop, the former skinhead rescued by Nawojczyk after a chance meeting on a downtown street. There is now a whole army of former gangbangers who owe their reformation, at least in part, to Steve Nawojczyk's stubborn resolve.

Nawojczyk's mission may have seemed daring and futile in the beginning. But God endowed him with an idea for good works and then gave him the will to proceed. In due course, He also gave Steve the means with which to achieve it.

20

—

What on Earth
Is It Now?

Not long after my father died in 1986, I started hearing that voice. To my dismay, it gave me the sense that I needed to try something different. Unfortunately, it did not explain what I needed to change, or when, why, or how. At first, I was intrigued. But when the voice kept at it without providing any of the details I would need in order to satisfy its demands, I became annoyed and decided to ignore it, chalking it up to some by-product of the grief I was still experiencing in the wake of my father's death. Despite my studious efforts to disregard the voice, it persisted. When I finally acknowledged that it was coming from you-know-who, I got angry.

Why on earth was He nagging me? I wondered. And why in the middle of my bereavement, when there was already so much to sort out. Hadn't I been faithful enough? When Daddy died, hadn't I accepted it as God's will, hadn't I rushed to His bosom for comfort rather than to the bottle or sulk in resentment and self-pity?

I decided to talk back to the voice.

Am I not already a decent child? Aren't I a hardworking woman, a hopelessly devoted mother, a good wife, a loyal daughter and sister, a regular churchgoer? And how am I supposed to squeeze anything else into my already crammed schedule? Into just what nanosecond of free time am I to fit this new assignment, which, I'll remind you, I cannot even begin to calculate since you, God, have not bothered to tell me what it is. Why don't you pick on someone else?

I let Him have it.

As every believer knows, however, God gives not only as good as He gets, but much, much, much better. He answered my complaints with not only more whispers, but also louder ones. And still, He withheld the particulars.

My response was to get even angrier. I'd show Him. For several weeks I avoided church altogether. Instead of getting up on Sunday mornings, I luxuriated in bed, taking my morning coffee and the newspapers there and flipping from one political talk show to the next. It was great in the beginning, but on my third Sunday out, I started to feel sick. I woke up with a pounding headache that day and in a sour mood. More sleep and analgesics took care of those, but a sense of shame crept into their place. I felt the same way the next Sunday and the one after that. By the sixth week of my boycott, I was whipped and ready to surrender. In a sobbing prayer, I apologized to God and told Him I was willing to accept the mission and would wait for

Him to fill in the blanks. The fog of headaches, moodiness, and shame lifted almost immediately. The next Sunday morning, I got up and went to church.

For the longest time thereafter, I continued my life as usual. Every now and then, I would go silent, hoping to hear that whisper, but nothing. Then, one afternoon at work, the voice piped up again. It said, simply, "Now."

For the life of me, I can't explain how I knew what "now" meant, but I sprang into action. On my way out the door to cover a city board meeting for the television news station where I worked as a reporter, I hastily wrote a letter of resignation, giving two weeks' notice. Without a word, I placed the letter on my news director's desk and took off for City Hall.

It is important to note here that none of this was anticipated. I had not discussed the prospect of quitting my job with my husband or children. I had not even turned the idea over in my own mind. I liked my job, felt at home in my workplace, and enjoyed a reputation for being good at what I did.

Nor was there a backup plan. As the mother of three young children with dental care, cars, and college in their future—not to mention daily meals—I needed a continuing source of income. Resignation would mean cutting off the only source I had, and if there were others in the offing, I didn't know what or where they were.

Nonetheless, I had not a sliver of doubt about the abrupt and mysterious decision I had made. In fact, a strange serenity settled over me and I remember marveling at how at peace I was, given the uncertainty of my future. I was not even surprised by my husband's reaction to the unexpected news. He always worried about the family finances; my impending unemployment would leave a big hole in the household purse. Yet when I told him what I had done, he responded with uncharacteristic calm. Why, he didn't even mention money. Rather, he reassured me that "everything will be all right," which, somehow, I already knew.

The man who wrote the media column for the state's leading newspaper had gotten wind of my resignation and called to ask about it. Predictably, he wanted to know why I was leaving. I told him I wasn't sure, that I just had a feeling it was time to go. Then he asked what I would do next. I told him I hadn't a clue. Then the strangest thing happened. The newspaperman told me the station's general manager had "shared" my resignation letter with him and he had found it "incredible; unbelievably moving." Would I mind if he ran an excerpt in his column? Befuddled but flattered, I gave him my okay.

Once the article appeared, I was besieged with calls from people who wanted to hire me, or at least explore the possibilities. Many were tempting, a few were odd and unappealing, one or two had the ring of dream jobs. But I turned every one of them down, all the while unsure of what I would or should do, but still not the least bit worried.

Just before my last day at the television station, a few of my colleagues took me out for a farewell lunch. On the way to the fancy restaurant they had chosen for the send-off, I happened to notice a clutch of old friends, all veteran print journalists, standing on a corner, waiting to cross the street. One of them was Bob McCord, a longtime newsman who is nationally known. Bob had been one of the big guns in the first newsroom I ever worked in. We hadn't talked in years.

Without thinking, I stuck my head out the window and yelled at my old editor. "Hey, Bob," I said. "I need to talk to you."

"Give me a call, then," he said.

God knows, I had nothing in mind when I asked for Bob McCord's ear. But when we spoke a few days later, a proposal came pouring out. I told him I wanted to start a column for his newspaper's op-ed page. Not the usual fare for the page—arms limitations agreements, inflation, and shuttle diplomacy—but pieces about the "little bombs that threaten people's lives every day." I wanted to write about making ends meet, homework overload, drug dealers in the neighborhood.

As soon as I said that, I winced, bracing for a polite but definitive "no thanks." After all, the *Arkansas Gazette*'s editorial and opinion section, called the Forum Page, was reserved for prestigious and recognized deep thinkers. It was there that two Pulitzer Prizes had landed to reward the paper's bold, insightful editorials during the turbulent desegregation of Little Rock Central High in 1957. The page had never featured anyone of my age—I was thirty-five—or my gender or my race. Plus, I was a television reporter and, back then, print journalists tended to look down their noses at a medium that routinely turned journalists into celebrities.

To my everlasting surprise, McCord greeted the proposition with enthusiasm. It was time for Arkansas's "old gray lady" to modernize, to "open up," to include new voices, he said. There was just one hitch: a new editor was coming in from Texas, a man who didn't know me from Adam, and he would have to approve the arrangement before we could proceed.

Two weeks later, I put on a good suit and met the *Gazette*'s newly arrived editor for lunch. He was a soft-spoken man with a dry wit and an inscrutable face. As I carried on like a runaway train, trying to dazzle him with my ideas for the proposed column, he betrayed no hint of what he was thinking. Exhausted by my own rambling, I finally shut up and got ready for something along the lines of *Well, it sounds wonderful and I'm sure you could write some interesting columns, but we want to keep the editorial and op-ed pages focused on serious, well-researched issues and I'm not sure you're up to that. But, I'll keep you in mind.*

No sooner had I stopped talking than the editor flashed a quick smile and said, "How many can you write a week and when can you start?"

This is what Bob McCord said about my column in his annual report to the readers of the Forum Page a few months after I began writing three pieces a week: "The greatest response from readers has come from the addition of the Deborah Mathis column. No feature—columns, comics, illustrations, etc.—ever added (or dropped) at any newspaper where I've worked has ever attracted so much attention."

The report continued: "Until very recently, 95 percent of all the opinion and commentary in the *Arkansas Gazette* (as well as virtually every other American newspaper) was written by middle-aged (or older), white, Anglo-Saxon males, usually ex-reporters who had lost their legs. Yet, 52 percent of our audience is female and 55 percent is 35 or under. Also, 19 percent of it is *not* white. So, as a baby boomer who is black and a married, working mother of three children, Deborah Mathis has a lot in

common with many of our readers. Her input into our newspaper is very valuable in making the *Gazette* what newspapers never used to be—truly representative of the people they serve."

I cannot say that I was divinely ordained to write the column, which began in 1988 and continues to this day—now in national syndication—nor that I am carrying God's word to readers nor that everything I write is right and righteous or pleasing to God. But I am certain that the advent and survival of the column are attributable to that long ago mysterious, inexplicable voice that first said "Do something else" and later said "Now." When I embarked upon this work, I had every intention of using the column to bring enlightenment, perspective, and a sense of community to the readership. Yet I know I have often flubbed the assignment, sometimes because of neglect, sometimes out of laziness, and sometimes out of ignorance. Nevertheless, I am sure it was by God that I got this forum. He's the one who planted the idea in my mind. He's the one who moved the decision makers like chess pieces on a board. The media reporter who first publicized my leave-taking at the television station? Bob McCord's immediate interest in my daring and unprecedented proposition? The new editor's surprise approval of an unknown's new idea for an old and revered paper whose prosperity was in his hands? The success of the column? It is all too much for mere coincidence.

That little voice is something else, I tell you. If we listen for it, then pay attention when we hear it, then heed and submit to it, God will take care of the rest. He will, as the young folks say, "hook you up." But you have to develop an ear for it. And there's the rub.

PART FIVE

❧

Answer

21

Love in Due Course

On the outside, Carla was tough as nails. She had to be. Her neighborhood was so overrun by ruffians that just walking home from school or the store or a friend's house could mean a run-in that ended in bruises and cuts and blackened eyes. By adolescence, Carla had grown tall and fit. But despite her luminous smile and pretty face, she was known as one of the meanest kids on the block. In fact, she made a conscious decision to adopt that persona at about age nine, when her little brother was beaten up and robbed of his brand-new bicycle on his birthday. Infuriated, she had scoured the neighborhood for the assailants and kept a lookout for days, and, at last, she spotted a kid on the bike one day, cruising along with two friends on foot. Without a word of warning, Carla had walked up to the rider and struck him hard in the chest, knocking him off the bike. In the fight that followed, Carla whipped the tar out of the boy who, not only injured but also humiliated, threatened revenge. Carla marched right over to the boy's house, knocked on the door, and told the boy's aunt what had happened. "If I ever see him again, I'm gonna mess him up," Carla told the woman. When the woman threatened to call the girl's father to protest the threat and her impudence, Carla stood her ground. "Call him and he'll whip *your* ass." That wasn't true. Carla's father was a hardworking man, a widower, who minded his own business and did his best to keep food on the table and a roof over the heads of his motherless children. But the bluff was effective. Even though she had a few more scraps with the young robber, kicking his butt each time, the boy eventually backed off, telling her he didn't want any more trouble from "your crazy family."

Despite the hard shell, Carla had a soft side, like most girls growing up in 1960s America. She liked to toy with makeup and spin records on the hi-fi and collect *Modern Romance* comic books. Although the women's movement helped buoy Carla's hopes of landing a good career someday, she also dreamed of falling in love, getting married, and having children, ensconced in a home of their own. In short, an upgrade of the proverbial happy-ever-after scenario.

When she was twenty, Carla met a guy who, she thought, might help her dreams come true. Robert was a looker, all right. The eyes, they were the clincher. They were so clear and piercing that Carla found it difficult to look at them for too long, lest they cast some kind of spell and make her lose her cool.

Not that she had much cool around Robert ever. He oozed self-assurance and his hair-trigger laugh, wry sense of humor, and coyness gripped Carla's fascination. Whenever she was around him, Carla's hard shell would dissolve so quickly that, after a while, she stopped even pretending to be anything but completely smitten. Naturally, then, she was elated when Robert announced that he was particularly drawn to her—there were so many women vying for his affections, after all—and Carla wasted no time letting him know that she was willing to be his, exclusively, setting aside all that she had heard, and some of what she had seen about Robert's reputation as a notorious ladies' man. She believed in "The One" theory—that for every person there is a perfect mate—and proceeded on the hope that the dynamic would hold true for her now.

It looked good in the beginning. Robert was attentive and ever-present. If there were other women, Carla figured, they couldn't be getting more than a conversation out of Robert, and a quick one at that, because between work and Carla, there wasn't any time for anything more. She watched him flirt every now and then, training those eyes on some blushing, giggling prey, but Carla rarely fussed about it. Robert had professed his love and commitment to her and seemed to mean it. Even Robert's old friends had often remarked about how "changed" he seemed. Allowing a few harmless flirtations seemed, to Carla, a fair way to thank the old Robert for the new one.

Robert and Carla were married one evening in 1973 in a simple ceremony in the home of Robert's parents. Many of Robert's longtime friends were still having a hard time imagining him settled down and married, but they toasted the newly-weds, who, indeed, seemed radiantly happy.

By the time the couple's baby boy was born not long afterward, Carla had gotten good and cozy with her role as keeper of hearth and home. But Robert was beginning to stray. He spent weekend evenings strolling the nightclub circuit and, more than once, Carla answered telephone calls from young women with breathy voices asking for "Robbie." When Robert's misbehavior became chronic, his wife angrily confronted him. "He kept talking about 'my freedom' and 'you're not going to control me' and that 'I'm the man' stuff," Carla recalled. The arguments grew louder and longer, then more frequent until, finally, they were "the only interaction we had," Carla says. "So I kicked him out."

From then on, Carla and Robert's relationship would keep a troubling rhythm: argument, separation, reconciliation, misconduct, argument, separation, reconciliation, misconduct, and so on. In the meantime, they had another son together.

During one spell, Carla threw in the towel and adopted the if-you-can't-beat-'em, join-'em strategy. For a time, she returned to the nightlife with Robert, but it wasn't long before that lifestyle took its toll. The late nights out left her bleary-eyed and exhausted at work; the family budget was being strained by the new overhead costs—babysitters and bar tabs and take-out meals. And, Carla believed, being a party girl was hurting her relationship with her children. She often found herself too tired, too moody—or too absent—to adequately attend to her growing boys' needs. Besides, her relationship with her husband was not improving. In fact, it was getting worse. Carla could feel her heart breaking, piece by piece.

• • •

"It all came crashing down one night," Carla remembers. "Robert was out in the streets, I didn't know how to find him, and the baby was sick. Then, too, Little Robert needed help on a school project he had to turn in the next day. I had to call my father, who had to get up out of his bed in the middle of the night to come and take the kids and me to the emergency room. So there I was at two o'clock in the morning, worried to death with a crying, sick baby and a sleepy-eyed child who had to go to school in a few hours and make a presentation, and a father who had worked all of his life and didn't need any more drama, and my husband was out running around somewhere. That was all I could take."

When Carla and the boys returned home several hours later, she found Robert sound asleep in their bed. "That sight made me so mad, I can't tell you," she says. "That old mean Carla started cooking up ideas. Should I pour ice water on him? Should I just jump on his back and beat him up in his sleep? Should I burn his clothes? I was just standing there listening to him snore and my chest was just heaving. I was just burning, I wanted to hurt him so bad."

Carla's wanton fantasies were suddenly interrupted by a gurgle from the sleeping baby still in her arms. "I looked down and he was kind of giggling in his sleep," she said. "I don't know what could have been going through his little mind, but it was the sweetest sound in the world. That little laugh just sent peace all through me."

Carla laid her baby in his crib and returned to the bedroom with a new plan. She fell to her knees.

"I just broke down and cried," she says. "I said, 'God, I

know I've been wrong, but please help me. I just want some peace. Please make Robert be the man he's supposed to be and I promise I will try to be the woman I'm supposed to be.'"

For the next several weeks, Carla put all of her energies into taking care of her children, doing her job, keeping the house. She continued to talk to God, repeating the pleas and the promises of that night, and watching her husband for signs of change. The weeks turned into months and nothing happened.

But Carla's prayers were being answered in other ways. Her faith was growing and so, now, was her pride and joy as she watched her sons mature into brilliant, honest, responsible young men. By his senior year in high school, the elder boy had been offered full academic scholarships from so many Ivy League schools that he and Carla had to have several sessions with school counselors to sort them all out. His little brother, two years behind, was following the same path. Both boys were exceedingly high achievers imbued with a sense of purpose and direction. Neither had ever caused their mother to worry or wonder about their whereabouts. Each had gotten part-time jobs on his own and willingly shared the proceeds with their mother.

Carla's sons are now both successful professionals with families of their own. They are, by all accounts, good husbands and fathers. And they have been superb sons, taking good care of their mother—and the father who has since mended his ways.

"It wasn't exactly what I prayed for, but it turned out better," Carla now says. "I asked God to make Robert the man he's supposed to be. I didn't know that he was going to make Little Robert the one. He was the one who brought me the peace and joy I was after—he and his little brother, Anton. And in time, their father came around, too. Like I said, it wasn't what I had in mind, but I had to learn to accept what God had in mind. And, you know something, it was a whole lot better plan than mine!"

22

—

Belonging

As a little girl, Betty Ann liked the small, cotton- and rice-farming town where she was born in the waning years of World War II. Despite the town's strict racial separateness, delineated by the matrix of tracks that accommodated four major railroad lines, she was a popular kid, favored for her quick wit, smart mind, and loquaciousness. Betty Ann was nothing if not outgoing and talkative. Always smiling, she was, for the most part, a happy girl.

But Betty Ann had problems. Her mother, Agnes, a pretty and lively unmarried woman, worked hard to provide for Betty Ann and her younger brother, Greg. But Agnes played hard, too. An occasional glass of scotch had long ago become a regular habit. In fact, by the time Betty Ann was an adolescent, Agnes was widely considered an alcoholic. In addition, the little family had no nearby kin. No grandparents or aunts or cousins to help Agnes and her children negotiate the bumps of life in

segregated, postwar, southern America. Betty Ann had known
her father only by name—Norman Miles, said to be a suave
and handsome man who had met and wooed Agnes during a
stint at a neighboring army base. Soon after Agnes got pregnant with Betty Ann, Norman had been deployed overseas and
the couple lost touch.

So it was that Betty Ann, naturally disposed to optimism
and precociously resourceful, learned early on that she would
have to pitch in to help rear Greg and tend the family hearth
and home.

The little town with its difficult circumstances could not
hold a girl like that for long. Betty Ann was a good student and
hoped higher education would spirit her away to another life, a
better life, in which she could develop her talents for writing
and might, one day, become a teacher.

Whatever her shortcomings as a mother, Agnes had at least
seen to it that her children were well fed, in school, and involved in church. In the beginning, she took them to a local
Baptist church. When they got older, she sent them on their
own.

Betty Ann flourished at the church, showing up regularly
for Sunday school, worship service, and Baptist Training
Union. She befriended the congregation and soon became a
favorite of the pastor, his wife, and their large, expanding family. In her teenage years, Betty Ann often earned a few dollars
babysitting Reverend and Mrs. Lawson's children. She loved
those times—the crush of people under one roof, the noise, the
bustle, the laughter. In a way, the Lawsons were like the family
she never had and for which she desperately yearned.

Just before Betty Ann graduated from high school, the Lawsons moved to a city 130 miles away, where Reverend Lawson had been chosen to pastor a larger and growing congregation. For a poor girl in the 1960s, her friends may as well have been moving across an ocean.

But the Lawsons had a plan. Their new city had a tiny college, supported by the Baptist Church and devoted to educating needy, determined, and talented young people like Betty Ann. If she lived with them, earning her keep as a babysitter and helpmeet around the house, she could get the college degree she so desperately wanted.

Agnes encouraged her daughter to take the offer, although Betty Ann was reluctant to leave her little brother and mother, whose health was in decline. But the girl realized that, if ever she was to break the poverty cycle and free herself and her family, this was the time. Late in the summer of 1961, Betty Ann packed a suitcase and boarded a southbound bus.

The Lawsons' new home was a huge, three-storied Victorian structure with cavernous rooms and a long, roomy front porch—far different from the cramped little quarters Betty Ann left behind in her railroad town. The front lawn was expansive and tree-studded. The back of the house spilled onto a wide carport and driveway. There was plenty of room for the newcomer.

According to routine, Betty Ann would help make breakfast for the Lawson brood in the morning, then hitch a ride with Reverend Lawson (or, occasionally, take a city bus) to the little college where she was enrolled as a freshman, majoring in education. She would be back in time to greet the youngest Lawson children when they got home from school and would supervise their afternoon chores, playtime, and homework.

The Lawsons' new neighborhood was awash in young children. Of the eighteen homes on the block, seven households had, like the Lawsons, two or more elementary-aged children. Those were the days before video games and *Sesame Street*, before drive-by shootings and street drug dealing. Kids played outdoors and got to know one another through rigorous games of hopscotch, dodge ball, double Dutch, bicycle races, and make-believe.

The three youngest Lawson children found their best playmates right next door in the daughters and son of another Baptist minister and his teacher-wife. Naturally, the next-door neighbors quickly got to know Betty Ann, whose sunny demeanor and high humor they found delightful.

One day, as the playmates refreshed themselves with Kool-Aid in the Lawson kitchen, Betty Ann asked one of the next-door neighbors her last name.

"Miles," the girl replied.

"Miles?" asked Betty Ann. "That's my real last name."

The little girl thought Betty Ann was pulling her chain.

"No it's not."

"Yes it is," Betty Ann said. "I go by Betty Ann Barnes, but my real last name—my father's last name—is Miles."

The little girl turned a skeptical eye on Betty Ann. She wondered whether the young woman was teasing her in some way, an elder having fun at a kid's expense.

"Uh-uh," the girl said again.

"I'm telling you the truth," Betty Ann said. "My real last name is Miles."

At the family dinner table that evening, the little girl told her parents what Betty Ann had said. Curiously, they did not dismiss the notion as far-fetched.

"What else did she say?" the father asked.

"That's all," the girl replied. "She just said her real last name is Miles."

The girl could not help but notice the glances shared by her parents. It was as if they were passing secret thoughts between them. It was enough to make the girl know she had to ask more questions.

Within a couple of days, the girl had more information to report.

"She said her father's name is Norman Miles and that he's in the service," the girl told her parents. "She said that he was overseas and that she lived with her mother."

Shortly thereafter, Reverend and Mrs. Lawson, Reverend and Mrs. Miles, and Betty Ann got together. And not long after that, Betty Ann was invited to the Miles home for dinner. There, she told her story of growing up in the small railroad, cotton, and rice town. Of being the firstborn and only daughter of Agnes Barnes, who had been romantically involved with Norman Miles but had never married him. Of having a younger brother, fathered by another man, whom she helped care for and rear. Of having met the Lawsons through church and moved in with them to pursue her education. Of having prayed long and hard for belonging, for a family.

As she talked, the Mileses could not help but notice the

striking resemblance between Betty Ann and members of their own family. She looked remarkably like Reverend Miles's own brother—and the brother's daughter, Clariece.

Reverend Miles donned his investigative hat and, within a few weeks, announced that Betty Ann Barnes, the girl next door, was indeed the daughter of his brother, Norman, by then a retired army sergeant living in Detroit.

The reunion of father and daughter took place within a few months. It was tearful and joyful and full of reminiscences. Norman and Betty Ann called Agnes, who cried with relief and thanksgiving. Clariece came to town from New York and posed for a picture with her younger half sister, the two arm-in-arm, with identical eyes, identical high cheekbones, identical smiles.

In due course, Betty Ann met an array of Miles relatives. Previously unknown uncles and aunts and cousins and a grandfather, patriarch of the family. Suddenly, she was surrounded by family, part of a network that ran coast to coast and that warmly and eagerly embraced the long-lost daughter.

"You don't know how hard I prayed for a family," an elated Betty Ann said at her first trip to a Miles family gathering in Kansas City. "I never thought this was how I would get it. God works in mysterious ways."

Today, Betty Ann is all Miles. And one of the family's favorites.

23

—

This Is a Test

The millions who tune in to professional football games on Sunday afternoons in the autumn and winter might know him as J.B. He likes it that way. The nickname implies a certain comfort level, a certain familiarity, a certain down-to-earthness that appeals to James Brown. That's James Brown the sportscaster, not the older, and very differently disposed, "godfather of soul."

J.B. is a tall, handsome, sturdily built man known for his friendliness and approachability—unusual traits for real celebrities among whose ranks J.B. humbly but authentically resides. Since 1994, he has anchored *Fox NFL Sunday,* the country's most-watched NFL pregame show. The ensemble of analysts and color commentators on the weekly national broadcast includes former Super Bowl–winning quarterback Terry Bradshaw, former Los Angeles Raiders defensive end Howie Long, and former Dallas Cowboys head coach Jimmy Johnson.

J.B. is living the good life these days. He dashes all over the country for pro football games, awards shows, speeches, and television specials. He has a beautiful, devoted wife and homes on both coasts. His suits are stylishly tailored. He is on the A-lists that comprise some of the country's most popular athletes and television executives. And as if the sports and entertainment world can't get enough of him, he is in steady demand to do even more.

Despite a grueling schedule, especially during football season, and the occasional longing for a quieter, simpler life, J.B. acknowledges that he has a good thing going. And to think, it almost didn't happen.

As a high school student in the mid-1960s, J.B. was a standout on the basketball court—not just at DeMatha Catholic High School in Hyattsville, Maryland, and not just in the region, but nationally. In his senior year, J.B. was named one of the five best high school basketball players in the country and, as a first-team all-American for two consecutive years, he was recruited by most of the nation's best college programs.

"I really admired these two African-American brothers who went to Columbia University—Jimmy McMillan and Hayward Dotson," J.B. said. "They were able to be athletically and academically successful." It was a reputation J.B. coveted and he proved his prowess in the classroom as well as on the ball court. In 1969, he accepted a full athletic scholarship to Harvard, the nation's oldest, and arguably its most prestigious, university.

J.B. was one of three hundred black freshmen enrolled at Harvard that fall. It was the largest incoming group of black students in the school's history, constituting one fourth of the freshman class. But it wasn't easy. The black students ran into resistance, low expectations, and, to some degree, alienation on the campus, and the tensions were exacerbated by the activist, outspoken nature of some black students who were sympathetic to, or affiliated with, such militant groups as the Black Panthers.

"Those were challenging times," J.B. recalled. "When I look back to when I was in high school and was being fed spiritually, I realize I left myself totally exposed in the collegiate environment. And quite frankly, I was not attending church. I was not being spiritually fed at those times. While I was certainly blessed to be at a school like Harvard, I didn't work as hard to stay on top as I had to get to the top."

He was never what most people would call a slacker, but compared to his ability and potential, J.B., by his own admission, did not make the most of his years at Harvard and getting by was becoming a way of life. When he graduated from Harvard in 1973, he was drafted by the Atlanta Hawks, but made a "disappointing" showing and was cut from the team. As he put it, "got cut; cried; came home; hid in the house for a couple of weeks."

"When I looked in the mirror, I couldn't fool myself. The bottom line was, I didn't do what I needed to do to make it ridiculously, painfully obvious that I was the best choice."

At that point, J.B. promised himself that he would "never ever again let an opportunity pass me by for lack of being prepared. I prayed to the good Lord to give me the discipline to do what I needed to do and to glorify Him. From that point forward, I had to make certain I did excellently because I recognized that, being an ambassador for Christ, people do watch."

J.B. began rebuilding. He landed a good position with Xerox, then managed a sales team with Eastman Kodak, all the while feeding his passion for sports by moonlighting as a broadcast announcer for the Washington Bullets (now Washington Wizards), a professional basketball team.

"My colleagues in corporate America thought I had absolutely lost my mind doing basketball games, making $250 a game, as opposed to being president of a division," he said. Burning both ends of the candle began to pay off when, while keeping his day job, J.B. began doing some work for Black Entertainment Television, then began announcing regional games, then started freelancing for CBS Sports. Later, he was hired as a local television sportscaster.

He was hooked and asked God to help him in his pursuit of a career in sports television. Still, J.B. worried that, at twenty-eight, he may have been too late a bloomer, given that so many broadcasters had entered the field straight out of college. Hatching a plan, J.B. paid news directors for critiques of his air tapes and set a five-year sink-or-swim deadline. "I asked God to help me understand if it was not meant to be."

But five years later "almost to the day," CBS offered J.B. a full-time job doing play-by-play for football and basketball games and a few anthology shows. At the time, the network held broadcast rights to most of the major sporting events. J.B., it seemed, was at the right place at the right time. "I was thought to be one of the young up-and-comers," he said.

But apparently not up and coming enough. In 1990, CBS

declined to renew the contract of its star sports broadcaster, Brent Musburger, who had been with the network for more than two decades and was known for his versatility at the sports mike.

"They had approached me and asked whether I would prefer being the lead play-by-play guy on college basketball or the lead guy hosting the studio show," J.B. recounted. "I told them I would be happy either way, though, if I had my druthers, I would have preferred play-by-play. But Jim Nash got play-by-play and the studio job went to Pat O'Brien. So there I was at another crossroads, crying my head off at home behind closed doors.

"Now, I'm saying to myself, 'If I can't get a lead position in basketball, which I *know,* maybe it's not meant for me. I remember my wife saying, go before the Lord and ask Him what is the deal because you've got to know that in the fullness of time, He will let you know what the game plan is and make use of your talent.' That's also the time my sister got on my case and looked at my tape and said, 'You know what? You don't articulate like you should.' So I went to Villanova for a voice coach, who broke down my tape, word by word. My sister was right. So my family told me to hang in because the Lord would make room for my talent."

As he was regrouping, however, J.B.'s employer was running into trouble. First CBS lost the NBA broadcast contract to ABC. Then it lost the NFL to Fox. As the major networks are wont to do, CBS had a regime change and brought in a new head of the sports division whose plans for J.B. involved only part-time gigs.

"I'm thinking, after all this time, Lord, you know how I've worked hard in this. It's in your hands. Fox had the contract. As the Lord worked it out, they were testing people for the studio show and it hadn't worked out for some of the people they had in there working with the strong personalities of Terry Bradshaw and Howie Long. And someone said, 'Why don't you give James Brown a chance?' They called me."

Since joining *Fox NFL Sunday,* J.B. has won two Sports Emmy Awards as best studio host and received the 1999 National Sportscaster of the Year award. He has also headlined sports specials on television and radio.

He takes none of his success for granted.

"Every Sunday before I go on the air, I make it a point to call my mother and my wife to have prayer with them. I know the power of prayer. All of these blessings that have happened to me personally and professionally, I have not a shadow of a doubt that God's hand was at work in this. I deliberately and studiously put myself in His hands and I am doing my level best to stay true to Joshua 1:8: *Let not this book of the law depart out of thy mouth, for thou shalt meditate both day and night.*

"Call me square if you want, but this is the way I've chosen to live my life. His book is the only one that says, 'Try me.' "

24

—

To Be Continued

The search for God continues. Actually, it's the search for evidence of God that has preoccupied humankind since every civilization has recognized His presence in one form or another.

This era is, of course, the most advanced to date. We have technologies and knowledge that exceed the wildest dreams and most far-fetched imaginations of our ancestors. Jules Verne and George Orwell may have been prescient, but modern realities have rendered their fantasies crude.

But modern advances have only frustrated the search for God. It seems that the more we are able to explain, the less we believe that the universe is the work of a supernatural creator, director, and caretaker who is invisible, immeasurable, and immortal. Our vanity tempts us to believe that our command of knowledge is the result of better-built brains (vis-à-vis evolution), and an extensive and enlarging information database. In other words, we have more to work with and we've gotten better at putting two and two together.

The human genome project is just one example of man's ability to harness information that earlier generations believed only God knew. We can explain so much now—and manipulate so much—that no wonder some believe, Who needs God?

Yet for people of faith, these imponderable achievements only underscore the belief that a greater power than man's is at large. The proud discoveries and inventions that win Nobel Prizes and headlines and fame are really only clues man has picked up that actually suggest, rather than dispute, the presence of God. In short, we are still hunter-gatherers: hunting for God, gathering clues along the way. And there's no telling what we don't know—not even enough to wonder about.

Consider, for example, this report in the July 11, 2003, *New York Times,* in which correspondent John Noble Wilford wrote:

> *In new observations of a distant region of primitive stars, astronomers have found the oldest known planet, a huge gaseous object almost three times as old as Earth and nearly as old as the universe itself.*
>
> *The discovery, based on measurements by the Hubble Space Telescope, challenged scientists to rethink theories of how, when, and where planets form. It is tantalizing evidence, astronomers said, that planets began appearing billions of years earlier than previously thought and so may be more abundant.*
>
> *Astronomers reported yesterday that the planet is more than twice as massive as Jupiter and is orbiting a pair of*

burned-out stars. It appears to have formed 12.7 billion
years ago, within a billion years of the origin of the uni-
verse in the theorized Big Bang.

Discovery of a new planet is a mind-boggling accomplishment, and it opens up another large can of questions—foremost among them, where it all came from. I learned the Big Bang theory in high school. It seemed feasible enough. But no one explained the origin of the gases and materials that ultimately collided, exploded, and imploded to produce the, literally, earth-shattering wallop. No one could then, nor can anyone now. The beginning of the beginning is still a mystery.

The landscape is so crammed and crowded with ego satisfactions and control factors now that it is only getting harder to keep an eye on the Big Picture: that there is an almighty and supernatural power whom we cannot understand, cannot measure, and cannot manipulate.

What about free will? Even if there is a God, say the skeptics, aren't human beings capable of self-determination? Don't we have choice? Aren't we responsible for ourselves?

I've wrestled with this conundrum for the longest time. I've found myself annoyed when someone says "See what God can do?" when a parking space opens up on a busy lot. Or when someone says "God got me dressed this morning." Then I would get annoyed by my own annoyance, wondering if it represented some unwelcome agnosticism.

After years of tangling with this, I have come to these conclusions: We are not robots being remotely controlled by a higher, unseen power. God is not the Wizard of Oz, pulling levers and pushing buttons from behind the curtain. God is not the ultimate micromanager or control freak. God allows us lots of leeway.

However, there *is* a master plan for our lives—a Big Picture, if you will—and the most important exercise of free will is to decide whether to submit to that plan or try to go it alone. If we choose the master plan, which ends in our salvation and reconciliation with God, then we are declaring that the choices we make will be in line with what pleases God. And that if we fall or fail, we will trust that He will forgive us, save us, dust us off, and set us back on track under His watchful eye. If we choose "our" way, we have elected to operate outside the bounds of God's grace. I believe a person can have great success and a happy life under either scenario. But with "our" way, the good times end with death. Likewise, a person can have sorrow and failure under either plan. But under the master plan, there is a protector, a defender, a comforter, a mind-mender, a friend on hand.

Accepting the concept of a divine master planner or author of destiny or a father of fate is difficult enough. But try wrapping the landlocked human mind around the proposition that we should accept God's will even when, by our standards, He did not deliver what we wanted.

Doubt nags me constantly. Not about the existence of God—of that I am certain. It's the doubt about what God can do that gets my goat. How do I dare even wonder after all I've seen? How I have envied the blessedly assured.

• • •

At the end of October 1988, a woman named Annette Thomas-Jones had a baby. Christopher Michael Anthony Jones was delivered earlier than expected—six weeks early—but that was not unusual for Annette, who had delivered both of her daughters prematurely.

The baby boy didn't quite reach four pounds at birth. But the hospital had one of the best neonatal facilities around, so while Christopher would need special care until he reached fighting weight, doctors were confident he would thrive.

Several times a day for the next two days, Annette received her baby for feedings and cuddling while she recovered from the Caesarean delivery. After an hour or two, a nurse would come in to take the baby back to the hospital nursery for tests and care.

The nurse who retrieved Christopher on the night of November 1 looked a little different from the others. She wasn't wearing an identification badge and she was dressed in white rather than pink like the rest of the staff. But her demeanor and movements were at least familiar, so Annette kissed her infant and passed him to the nurse, who promised to return him after a trip to the nursery for weighing.

But the nurse never came back with Christopher. Indeed, she was no nurse at all, but rather a baby-snatcher. The woman, later identified as Acqunetta Rushon Smith, lived about seventy miles away. Smith had told her boyfriend she was pregnant with his child, hoping the news would draw a commitment from him. But Smith was not pregnant. A friend of hers said she was convinced Smith had been pregnant and miscarried, but Smith's doctor said not.

For several days, police were on the lookout for the phony nurse and baby Christopher. Medical professionals appeared on television, issuing appeals for the abductor to return the child, emphasizing his delicate condition as a preemie.

But in every interview with reporters, Annette was unusually calm. She kept saying she knew God was watching over her baby. Every time, she expressed confidence that God would settle the situation.

I remember clearly that the young mother's cool under the circumstances was so unusual that, for a bit, there were buzzes that she, or maybe her husband, had something to do with the baby's disappearance. That's how rare real faith is, the kind that holds up under pressure. People didn't recognize it, or accept it, when they saw it.

Indeed, it must have been a real test for the Joneses. But they passed it. Two weeks after their ordeal began, the family had Christopher back. Not only was he unharmed, he had put on weight. Annette's expressed faith had paid off. She could thank dedicated law enforcement officials, diligent reporters, and a vigilant public for Christopher's safe recovery. But she knew whom to thank first. "Praise the Lord, hallelujah" was Annette's initial reaction when she learned her baby had been found.

There are plenty of other stories that buttress faith in God, or should. In St. Petersburg, Florida, Roger Clay's parents were sadly approaching the fifth anniversary of his death in a motor-cycle accident when a stranger called to say that he had something for them. The caller had just come upon a message in a bottle that read, "To whoever finds this letter, please write me a letter and let me know." Roger had written it fourteen years earlier and set the bottle adrift in the Gulf of Mexico. Because he had included his address at the time, the stranger had been able to track down Roger's parents. As Lisa Clay told a reporter, "Here I was, trying to escape Roger's death, and he reaches out and gives me this message, this gift." Said his father, "It was like he was trying to remind us he was still with us."

And there's the man who lay in a coma for nineteen years while his baby girl grew into a young woman and his mother grew old. And one day he just woke up and started talking again. His doctors expect him to recover fully.

And there's the miracle at the Quecreek mine in Pennsylvania, in which nine miners, trapped underground with rising water and sinking oxygen levels, emerged whole, to the man, stunning even the experts.

I have seen all of these miracles, these wonders, not to mention the countless ones that have relieved or saved me through the years.

Yet every time I am faced with a new challenge or a new threat—to my peace of mind, if nothing else—I find myself wondering anew whether God will come through this time.

What a shame. If anyone should know by now, it's me. In this department, I am most definitely a slow learner.

• • •

Aside from the doubt, I am such a backslider, such a half-stepper. Like the child away in college who only calls home when the vittles are getting low, I have too often gone down on my knees only in a time of emergency. And like the loving parent that He is, God has taken the call every time—why, I can't say, given my disloyalty.

In addition, I, like a lot of believers, have the audacity to be picky about my blessings. Too often, when we ask for God's help, we put in a detailed requisition, instructing Him on how to fix our problems. This, of course, flies in the face of professed submission to God's will. It implies a provisional acceptance of God's will. As long as the blessing materializes as we proposed it—if it fits our specifications—then we will give the credit to God.

By applying such conditions, however, we not only undermine God's will (and contradict our pledge of allegiance to it), but we also tend to cloud our vision so that we do not see Him working in a way, in a place, and at a time of His choosing.

If we really believe that God hears us and knows what He's doing, then our prayers and supplications should be simple: Lord help me through this and help me accept your will.

I've tried to teach this to my children, who may not be aware that their mother is preaching to herself as well. There's an old saying about "preaching to the choir." But as a former choir director and choir member, I know those of us who lift our voices to the Lord need to hear the sermon, too.

Allison, my middle child, was having some problems at the culinary school she attended. For the first several months, all

was well. But these latest courses were difficult, highly techni-
cal, and being taught by a man who was known as a stern
taskmaster. On several occasions, Allison and the instructor had
bumped heads. According to her, he seemed impatient with
students who didn't get everything on the first go-round. Allison began to despair that she would fail the course.

"I just want to warn you that I don't think I'm going to do
well in this unit," she told me. "I might not pass it. I know I'm
not going to be ready for practicum."

Naturally, I tried to keep my daughter's spirits aloft, re-
minding her to do the best she could and reassuring her about
the timetable for completion. "If you have to take the course
over, you'll take it over," I told her. Still, I could tell that was of
little comfort to Allison. She wanted to pass the class.

"I just wish I could start over," she said, noting that the
four-week unit was already halfway done. She promised to
pray over it. "Then you'll have to accept however God works it
out," I added. "I know," she said.

Shortly thereafter, I noticed a pronounced change in Allison's tone of voice. She sounded like her old cheerful self.

"Are things working out in that class?" I inquired.

"Not really," she said. "I mean, the chef and I are getting
along much better. We had a good talk. But I'm still thinking I
might not pass the class."

"I've told you not to worry about that. You can take it over."

"Yeah, but Ma, that's going to stretch out my time even
more, and that's going to cost you money."

"Oh, honey, we're not going to worry about that, okay?
You just do the best you can. You prayed over it, right?"

"Yes."

"And what did I tell you about accepting His will."

"You're right. Okay. I'm going to accept whatever happens."

"After you do the best you can and turn it over to God, that's all you can do. Except trust, you've got to trust."

"I will."

In the middle of the third week of the course, Allison called me, excitedly, in the middle of the day.

"What are you doing at home?" I asked.

"We were sent home," she said.

As Allison explained it, the chef had been waiting for a shipment of food and materials needed to demonstrate various cooking techniques to the class and which the students needed to practice for their final exam. The shipment was supposed to have arrived before the new unit began and, for weeks, the chef had been stalling.

The morning of the day Allison called, a large truck pulled up to the school. A team of chefs and school officials met the driver at the delivery port, ready to give him the third-degree about his extreme tardiness. When the driver opened the truck's big double doors, a powerful stench rushed out. Upon inspection, the chefs discovered that every bit of the food inside was spoiled and unusable.

"They dismissed the class and told us they would call each student tonight after deciding what to do about this," said Allison.

The next morning she called to report that school officials had found nothing salvageable in the shipment and, therefore, were unable to proceed with classes.

"They told us to take the rest of the week off," Allison said.

"We'll go back Monday and, guess what? We're going to start the class from scratch."

I'm sure when she had prayed for help with her dilemma, Allison had a particular remedy in mind. Maybe the chef would quit. Maybe he would just decide, out of the goodness of his heart, to give befuddled students a break. Maybe Allison would suddenly have clarity, an epiphany, about every aspect of her studies and then ace her tests. She had not even thought about spoiled food being her deliverance.

Which is another reason it is foolish to prescribe our own cure. God is more imaginative than we are, to put it mildly. And if you'll pardon the understatement, He has more resources than we do. Some of them can be right under our noses.

An old joke goes something like this:

A flood is threatening a small town, so the sheriff's deputies go door to door advising people to evacuate their homes and businesses. People readily obey. But when the deputies get to Mr. John Doe's house, he refuses to vacate.

"I'm not leaving," he says. "The Lord will take care of me."

The next day, the deputies return in a boat to Mr. Doe's house. The water is already up above the man's front porch.

"Mr. Doe," they say, "you've got to get out now. The water is still rising."

"I'm not leaving," he says again. "The Lord will take care of me."

Another day passes, the flood is worsening and the deputies take another boat to the Doe home, where the entire bottom half of the house is underwater. They spot Mr. Doe looking out of a second-floor window.

"Mr. Doe," they shout, "come with us now or you'll drown."

"I'm not leaving," Mr. Doe shouts back. "The Lord will take care of me."

By the next day, the water has swallowed Mr. Doe's house. Deputies return in a helicopter and find the old man on his roof. They drop a lifeline.

"This is your last chance, Mr. Doe," the deputies call out. "Grab the rope and we'll take you to safety."

"I'm not leaving," Mr. Doe yells. "The Lord will take care of me."

When the deputies flew over the next day, there was no sign of Mr. Doe. His body washed up a few days later.

At the gates of heaven, Mr. Doe asked St. Peter for a private audience with God.

Standing before God, Mr. Doe thanked the Lord for the bountiful blessings of his life on Earth. But he had one question.

"That flood," he said. "I was expecting you to save me, God. Why did you allow me to drown?"

God studied Mr. Doe for a moment, then said, "I sent you two boats and a helicopter, what more did you want?"

And that's it, isn't it? It's that we underestimate God's power, His wit, and His will. It's that we wait for God to make the river dry up and end up missing the boat.

It Is No Secret (What God Can Do)

(Music and lyrics by Stuart Hamblin)

The chimes of time ring out the news
Another day is through.
Someone slipped and fell.
Was that someone you?

You may have longed for added strength,
Your courage to renew.
Do not be discouraged,
For I bring hope to you.

It is no secret what God can do.
What He's done for others, He'll do for you.
With arms wide open, He'll pardon you.
It is no secret what God can do.

There is no night, for in His light
You never walk alone.
Always feel at home,
Wherever you may roam.

There is no power can conquer you
While God is on your side.
Take Him at His promise,
Don't run away and hide.

It is no secret what God can do.
What He's done for others, He'll do for you.
With arms wide open, He'll pardon you.
It is no secret what God can do.

About the Author

Deborah Mathis, a veteran broadcast and print journalist, is the author of *Yet a Stranger: Why Blacks Still Don't Feel at Home.*